Received On:

MAR 2 6 2011

Ballard Branch

D0975772

NO LONGER PROPERTY OF
SEATTLE PUBLIC LIBRARY

Red Dust Road

Red Dust Road

An Autobiographical Journey

Jackie Kay

ATLAS & CO. *New York*

Copyright © 2010 by Jackie Kay

First published in the United Kingdom by Picador, an imprint of Pan Macmillan, a division of Macmillan Publishers Limited.

All rights reserved. No portion of this publication may be reproduced or transmitted in any form or by any means, electronic or mechanical, including photocopy, recording, scanning, or any information or storage retrieval system, without permission in writing from the publisher, except in the case of brief quotations embodied in critical articles and reviews.

"One for My Baby (And One More for the Road)" from the motion picture *The Sky's the Limit*. Lyric by Johnny Mercer. Music by Harold Arlen. ©1943 (Renewed) by Harwin Music Co. All rights reserved. Reprinted by permission of Hal Lenoard Corporation.

This is a true story. However, in order to protect privay, some names and places have been changed.

Atlas & Co. Publishers
15 West 26th Street, 2nd floor
New York, NY 10010
www.atlasandco.com

Distributed to the trade by W. W. Norton & Company

Printed in the United States

Atlas & Co. books may be purchased for educational, business, or sales promotional use. For information, please write to info@atlasandco.com.

Library of Congress Cataloging-in-Publication Data is available upon request.

ISBN: 978-1-935633-34-1

15 14 13 12 11 1 2 3 4 5 6

For my family,

With love

All biographies like all autobiographies
like all narratives tell one story
in place of another.

Hélène Cixous

The past is never past.

William Faulkner

The last big rains of the year were falling.
It was time for treading red earth
with which to build walls.

Chinua Achebe

Nicon Hilton Hotel, Abuja

Jonathan is suddenly there in the hotel corridor leading to the swimming-pool area. He's sitting on a white plastic chair in a sad cafe. There's a small counter with a coffee machine and some depressed-looking buns. He's dressed all in white, a long white African dress, very ornately embroidered, like lace, and white trousers. He's wearing black shoes. He's wired up. My heart is racing. 'Jonathan?' I say.

'Yes,' he says, standing up and turning slowly to meet me.

I hadn't meant to meet him here. I'd been sitting in the swimming-pool area at a nice table by the bar, waiting for two hours, looking up at every elderly man coming through the opening in the wall. It's a strange thing, looking at one black man after another wondering if he is your father. It seemed this morning that everyone was. Several handsome men appeared, all of an age with Jonathan, wearing more and more elaborate outfits in all sorts of vivid colours – bright green, bright blue, burnished gold, tangerine orange. It was like sitting watching a fashion show of old black men walk the gangway to the pool bar.

Each one made some kind of entrance, it seemed, because each one could have been my father.

I wasn't sure that the staff at the hotel reception would definitely pass on my message to send him to the pool bar, so I kept going back to check. Jonathan had said he would arrive sometime in the afternoon.

Everybody told me that afternoon in Nigeria could be anything between noon and 5 p.m. I went to the reception and asked if anybody had called for me. 'No, nobody,' they said. Then I rushed to my room to check again by phoning the hotel operator. 'Yes,' she said, 'somebody called for you.'

'When?'

'About three minutes ago,' she said.

I tore along the corridor and pressed the lift button. Downstairs I saw the man in white sitting in the odd little cafe. It's the first time I've ever seen anybody sit there since I got here yesterday.

'Can we go straightaway to your hotel room?' he asks me.

'Can we go to my room?'

'Yes, I would like to go to your room now.'

We walk along the corridor to the lift and all the lights suddenly go out. Another power   ̱e his hand and lead him towards the lift in the dark. I grope about in the darkness holding my father's hand. Then the lights suddenly come back on again and we get into the lift. He doesn't talk. I know he won't talk until he gets into the room. He doesn't look at me. He looks down at his black shoes and clasps his hands. He's carrying a plastic bag. A white plastic bag. When I met my mother, she was also holding a plastic bag. Both my birth parents, on first sight, looked like some homeless people look, who carry important papers in carrier bags.

I had been told they met in 1961 in the dance hall in Aberdeen. Jonathan was a student there and my mother was a nurse. They kept in touch during my mother's pregnancy, then Jonathan returned to Nigeria and my mother went to a mother-and-baby home in Edinburgh to have me. I was adopted five months later by a couple in Glasgow – the people who are to me my real parents. They are lifelong and committed socialists. When I traced my birth mother some years ago I discovered that after her relationship with Jonathan, she had become a Mormon. The Latterday Church of Jesus Christ Saints or whatever. The Mormons, she told me, believe that adopted people cry out to be adopted while they are still in the womb. When I told my mum that my mother was a Mormon, she said, 'Oh, Jesus, that's the pits. Why not have a wee half bottle and forget all about it.'

And now we're in the room. I'm about to have a conversation with my birth father for the first time.

Jonathan is moving about from foot to foot, shifting his weight from side to side, like a man who is about to say something life-changing. He begins: 'Before we can proceed with this meeting, I would like to pray for you and to welcome you to Nigeria.' I feel alarmed. Extreme religion scares the hell out of me. It seems to me like a kind of madness. But it is obvious to me that Jonathan won't be able to talk at all if I try and skip the sermon. So I say, 'OK, then,' and he says, 'Sit, please.' And I sit.

He plucks the Bible from the plastic bag. Then he immediately starts whirling and twirling around the blue hotel room, dancing and clapping his hands above his head, then below his waist, pointing his face up at the ceiling and then down to the floor, singing, 'O God Almighty, O God Almighty, O God Almighty, we welcome Jackie Kay to Nigeria. Thank you, God Almighty, for bringing her here safely. She has crossed the waters. She has landed on African soil for the very first time. O God Almighty!' He does some fancy footwork. He is incredibly speedy for a man of seventy-three. He's whirling like a dervish. Suddenly, he takes off his shoes and puts them on my bed and kneels on the floor and reads the first of many extracts from the Bible. He seems to half read and half recite them; he appears to know the Bible by heart. As he recites he looks at me directly, quite a charming look, slightly actorish. The sermon for him is a kind of performance; his whole body gets thrown into it.

'God has given you this talent. You are a writer. You have written books. You have been blessed. God already knows about you. Don't think for a second that God hasn't been waiting for you. Now all you must do is receive Christ and your talent will become even bigger and you will become more focused. Amen. From this moment on you are protected. God protects the talented. Amen. You can walk through fire, you won't get burnt. You can swim

4

in dangerous waters, you won't drown. Don't even bother with your hotel safe. God is looking out for you.'

I shift uneasily in my seat. Christ Almighty, my father is barking mad. He spins and dances and sings some more, singing in the most God-awful flat voice, really off-key. The singing sounds like a mixture of African chanting and hymns. It's a shock. Despite the fact that he can't sing, his performance is captivating. I watch his bare feet dance round the room and recognize my own toes. He looks over directly into my eyes again to see if I'm persuaded. 'I see in your eyes that you are not yet able to put your full trust in God. And yet you know that that would make me happy. At every reading you do, you could take the message of our Lord. Think of the people you could convert.' (I think of the twelve people at a reading in Milton Keynes Central Library on a rainy Thursday night.)

'Think of all the people you could bring to the Lord if you get ready to receive Christ.' I look as noncommittal as possible. I start to think that I should try and get this to stop. It feels like a kind of assault. He senses me thinking this and says, 'Just one more extract from the Bible. I prayed to God you would be attentive and you are being attentive. I prayed to God you would be patient and you are being patient.'

He wants me to be cleansed, cleansed of his past sin. 'If animal blood can cleanse sins under the Old Law, how much more can the blood of Jesus Christ cleanse us and prepare us for glory?' As Jonathan says this, his eyes seem to light up from behind like a scary Halloween mask.

'For if the blood of bulls and of goats, and the ashes of a heifer sprinkling the unclean, sanctify the purifying of the flesh, how much more shall the blood of Christ, who through the eternal Spirit offered himself without spot to God, purge your conscience from dead works to serve the living God?'

I realize with a fresh horror that Jonathan is seeing me as the sin, me as impure, me the bastard, illegitimate. I am sitting here, evidence of his sinful past, but I am the sinner, the live embodiment of his sin. He's moved on now, he's a clean man, a man of glory and of God, but I'm sitting on the hotel room chair little better than a whore in his eyes, dirty and unsaved, the living proof of sin. Christianity has taken away his African culture and given him this. I'm thinking about colonialism and missionaries and not properly listening. I hear his voice in the background. God knows how long it has all been now.

I keep trying to rouse myself to ask him kindly to stop. 'And from Jesus Christ, who is the faithful witness and the first begotten of the dead, and the prince of the kings of the earth. Unto him that loved us, and washed us from our sins in his own blood. And hath made us kings and priests unto God the father; to him be glory and dominion for ever and ever. Amen.' I've zoned out now, drugged by his voice. I go in and out of consciousness like somebody who's very ill. I can't see properly. Pages of the Bible are flying around the room like hummingbirds. I am desperate for a drink. My glass of wine is sitting on the table in front of me, but it seems disrespectful to drink alcohol in the middle of my own personal service.

'Thank you for your patience,' Jonathan says again after another half-hour facing up to eternity. The tears are pouring down my face. I can't stop. It's a flood. It's self-pity. Jonathan is delighted to see them. He thinks maybe I am ready to receive Christ. He thinks I'm moved by his sermon. I am moved; my cheeks are soaking wet. I wipe them with my bare hands as Jonathan's voice goes deep and he lifts his hands into the air and claps and spins like a windmill. I think maybe it's nearly over.

Dear God; I'll believe in you if only this will stop. I look at my watch. He's been praying for a solid hour. The man can talk. We have that in common too. 'I prayed you would be docile. Thank you for paying attention.' I shuffle in my seat ready to get up. Then he starts up again, more whirling and twirling and shouting to God Almighty. More clapping and foot-tapping and spinning and reciting. A whole big wad of the Bible rolls out of his mouth like ectoplasm.

'For the grace of God that bringeth salvation hath appeared to all men, teaching us that, denying ungodliness and worldly lusts, we should live soberly, righteously, and godly in this present world. Open your heart to him. Repent of your sins. Allow me to purify and cleanse you. I want to pour out my glory. Believe what I am telling you.'

I try to think of all my sins. True, there are a lot of them. But the fact that I was born out of wedlock? That is not my sin.

Jonathan still wants me to receive Christ. 'You won't give me that assurance? Why won't you give me that assurance?' I don't reply at first because I'm not sure I'm supposed to answer. Then there is a tiny moment's silence where I say: 'I would like you to respect my beliefs as I respect yours. I'm not comfortable with being born again.' I don't want to hurt his feelings and if I told him that I was an out-and-out brutal atheist he'd have to sit down. Even if I said I was an agnostic, he'd feel dizzy. He tells me of meeting a man on the way to the Nicon Hotel in Abuja who was a non-believer and how much of a blow to him this man was, how he'd had to get away fast before the man pulled his spirits down.

Jonathan needs believers; he needs believers like some people need cocaine. He needs the fresh hit, the new blood of a beginner believer. I start to see him as a kind of holy vampire, dressed in white, ready to take me in, to help me receive Christ. There's not even a wee wafer or anything in the room. 'God has intended us to meet after I became a born-again Christian. We should deliberate on the issue of new birth. Your talents are even greater than mine. You are going to be very big and God is going to help you. All you have to do is receive Christ and everything will blossom from there. Your whole career. You won't believe the big changes that are going to be happening to you.' He's desperate. He's trying to bribe me with my own career! The writer in me perks up for a couple of sick, ambitious seconds. Nope – not even for my writing could I receive Christ. My head is pounding, a tight headache as if somebody has been banging nails into my forehead. Perhaps I'm being crucified! 'So the people shouted when the priests blew with the trumpets; and it came to pass, when the people heard the sound of the trumpet, and the people shouted with a great shout, that the wall fell down flat, so that the people went into the city. Do you see it? Are you ready to take your city and our land for Jesus? Repent now of every single sin in your life. Receive healing. Follow the six steps to Salvation: Acknowledge, Repent, Confess, Forsake, Believe, Receive.' He has the whole list of extracts written down on a tiny scrap of lined paper which begins with 'Welcome Jackie Kay to Nigeria' in blue biro (chapter such and such, verse such and such). He starts up again. He's like a bad poet who doesn't know when to quit, reading one poem after another to a comatose audience. I think, Oh, fuck it, let me drink that wine. I reach out and knock the whole glass back in one gulp. It's been two hours, two hours of non-stop praying. I'm exhausted. All the blood has drained out of my face. I can feel how pale I must look. My father has drunk my blood.

I say: 'You definitely know your Bible,' and he beams with pride. There is clearly no compliment I could pay him that would be higher than that, except perhaps, 'You're a good-looking man for your age.'

And then all of a sudden it stops like the rain at the end of the rainy season. Jonathan sits down, shattered. 'I thank you again for your patience. And now the time is yours. I will eat with you. I will have a drink with you.

I will stay for as long as you like. I am in no particular hurry.' I have a terrible headache; the idea of spending an indefinite period of time with my father is not now as attractive as it was on the aeroplane.

At the bar, I knock back another glass of wine and ask him if he is glad to meet me. 'Yes,' he says, 'because you are evidence of my past. Once I used to go clubbing and such, and drink wine and meet women and now I am a preacher. You are my before; this is my after. You are my sin, now I lead this life.' Sin again, how dreary it is to go on and on about sin. 'You obviously have my genes. None of my children are dullards. Not one of them. But if people were to know about you, they would lose their faith in God,' Jonathan says. Goodness, I think, I never knew I was that powerful. 'The only way I could be open about you would be if I was able to showcase you, and you agreed to be born again. Then I would take you to the church and say, "This woman is my daughter. She is my before. This is my after." But you have given me no assurance that you would receive Christ and even if you did I would still have to think about how all this would affect God. I have discussed it with God and God agrees with me that for the time being it is best to keep quiet about this. I have told nobody that I was coming here to see you today. I have not told my young wife. My wife is also high up in our church. She is head of the women, I of the men. If I was going to tell anybody I would tell her.'

So I'm a secret, a forty-year-old secret, and must remain one unless I accept the Lord. I'm surprised that it seems so difficult for him to tell his wife, given that she was not married to him at the time. 'What age is she?' I ask.

'She is your age,' he says. 'God – in his wisdom – has provided somebody for my sex drive. We are trying for a baby.' I like that: God – in his wisdom – has provided somebody for my sex drive.

'You are seventy-three!' I say.

'So? A man can do it at any age,' he shrugs. 'God would like us to have another baby.'

How lovely it must be to believe in such a God, to hide your past in God's name, not to feel a second's guilt. To be religious in this way must be great fun. When I tell my mum about it on the phone, down the incredibly clear line from Abuja to Glasgow, how he doesn't want to tell any of his children, and how I must remain a secret, how he feels I am his past sin, she says: 'By God, did we rescue you!'

1969

I am seven years old. My mum, my brother and I have just watched a cowboy and Indian film. I'm sad because the Indians have lost again, and I wanted them to win. It suddenly occurs to me that the Indians are the same colour as me and my mum is not the same colour as me. I say to my mum, Mummy why aren't you the same colour as me? My mum says, Because you are adopted. I say, What does adopted mean. My brother scoffs; Don't you know what adoption means? I can't believe you don't know what adoption means. He's eating a giant-size bowl of cornflakes. He eats cornflakes for nearly every meal. No, I don't know. I'm nearly in tears. I've heard the word before but I don't really understand it. My mum says, It means I'm not really your mummy. What do you mean, you're not really my mummy? I say. I am crying for real now because I love my mum so much and I want her to be my real mummy and I'm worried she means she is not real and that something is going to happen to her, that she is going to disappear or dissolve. She says, Your real mother couldn't keep you so she gave you to me so that I could be your mummy. Yes, and that means you're not really my sister, my brother laughs. Ha ha. Do you get it? Are you making this up? I ask my mummy. Is this one of your stories? She's so good, my mummy, at telling stories. No, it isn't, she says. She's in tears herself too. It's upset her. Your real daddy came from Nigeria in Africa and your mummy came from the Highlands. What, I say, so my daddy isn't my real daddy either? No, my mum says. I'm distraught. I can't stop crying. I love them both so much the idea that people I have never met are my real parents and not them is horrible. How long have you known about this? I ask my brother, furious with him for some reason because he's laughing and finds the whole thing very funny. I've known for ages. I can't remember not knowing, he says. So it's good, isn't it? You're not my real sister. Ha! Ha! My mum goes out of the room and comes back and wipes her face on a tea towel. She says, But your dad and I love you more than all the tea in China, more than all the waves in the ocean and will love you till all the seas run dry. And you are special. You were chosen. And everyone needs cuddles to survive. Everyone needs cuddles, so they do. Come here and let your mummy give you a big cuddle.

Christchurch to Glasgow

My mum and dad met in Christchurch in the South Island
of New Zealand, though my mum comes from Lochgelly
in Fife, and my dad from Townhead in Glasgow. I've often
wondered if they would ever have met had they not both
ended up on the other side of the world, in the southern
hemisphere, enticed by the completely free fare, in the
days when Australia and New Zealand were determined
to increase their working population, and by the adven-
ture of the journey. My mum was eighteen when she left
for New Zealand and my dad was twenty-five. They met
in 1952 in a place called the Coffee Pot, where my mum
had a waitressing job. 'Your dad used to come in there
with all his climbing mates, Blondie, Wattie . . . – I can't
remember the rest of their names, a good-natured big
crowd – I think he liked me because I gave him big por-
tions. Isn't that right, John? Then he asked me out on our
first date. Why did you ask me out? Did you fancy me?'
My dad, even at the age of eighty-four, seems a little
embarrassed at my mum's flirtatiousness, and will never
just say, 'Yes, I fancied you.' Though he always will say,
'Oh, your mother was a good-looking woman, no doubt

about it.' And she'll say, 'A catch, was I a catch?' And he'll say dubiously, 'Yes . . . a catch, quite a catch,' as if that doesn't quite capture it for him, and he's being jostled into the wrong word.

My parents married in 1954, the same year the Supreme Court ruled that race-based segregation in schools was unconstitutional, the same year that Senator Joseph McCarthy conducted nationally televised inquiries into the communist infiltration of the army, the same year that there was massive interest in Billy Graham's Christian revival meetings; the same year as the first Annual Newport Jazz festival where later Miles Davis would blow the crowd away with his live performance of 'Round Midnight'.

My mum often tells me the story of their first date. 'He turned up in a big truck, a big filthy truck to take me out for our first date,' my mum says.

'Plenty of women would have been impressed with a truck like that,' my dad says. 'No many people had wheels in those days.'

'A big filthy truck,' my mum repeats. 'I had to climb up into it.'

'We went to the movies,' my dad says, moving on, 'we went to see *Death of a Salesman*, quite a classy film for our first date. Do you remember, Ellen?' (My dad calls my mum Ellen.) 'That it was *Death of a Salesman*?'

My mum nods, not as proud of this as my dad, impatient to get back to the romance of it all. 'I think he was in love with me. Were you in love with me, John?'

'Willy Loman was played by Fredric March. He was quite something, but no as good as Alf Garnet that time when we saw it in the Kings. Do you remember that, Jackie? That performance by Alf Garnet was a revelation.'

I nod. 'I took my friend Aileen Spence.'

'So you did, so you did. I'd forgotten she came along.' There's a great pleasure at eighty-four to be had in recouping lost memories, netting little bits in; they sparkle and please, tiny silver fishes.

'We were married about six months after we got engaged, weren't we, John?'

'Only six months?' I ask. Somehow, even though I've been told this story of my parents' meeting in New Zealand many times, each time a new bit surfaces that I hadn't noticed before.

'No point hanging around when you're sure,' my mum says with an air of sophistication. 'Plus I didn't like my flatmate.'

'That's more like it! It had nothing to dae wey romance. You just didnae like yer flatmate! Was I duped or what?' my dad says, enjoying the idea that he might have been tricked into marrying my mum.

'How romantic is this?' my mum says. 'Your dad said to me – what would you prefer, a wedding ring or a rucksack, because we canny afford both? I chose a rucksack.'

'Good for you,' I say again as I've said when I've heard that story before. 'That's quite cool,' I say, 'don't you think?'

My dad shrugs. 'Not so much cool as practical. A ring doesnie help you to go on a walking holiday.'

'It was a good quality rucksack, lasted years. Before we got married I bought myself a wedding ring for three pounds. I bought it from a second-hand shop. I got quite attached to it. But my hands have got that thin that the other week it just slipped off when we were away in Shetland, and I didn't notice it going. I was distraught.'

'Why were you distraught when you chose it yersell?' my dad jokes.

'You attach value to things, emotional value to things!' my mum says and laughs as if human beings are all crazy.

'That's capitalism for you!' my dad says and laughs too. 'We're all mugs. We've all got a wee bit of Willy Loman in us. That woman that played Linda in the film, Mildred Dunnock, she was brilliant too.'

'Maybe it wasn't losing the ring that upset me,' my mum says. 'Maybe it was my fingers getting thinner. Maybe it was just getting old.'

My parents married on the day after April Fool's Day in 1954. The day before my dad had fallen through the office floor, when he was working for CWF Hamilton and Company, an accident that had reminded him of an earlier one when he was just fourteen and working for Mavor and Coulson Ltd, which made mining machinery. The gaffer had asked my dad to climb onto his desk to get something and he'd knocked over a stone jar of ink. This earned him the nickname Inky. I remember loving it when my dad's old climbing pals called him Inky. The proof of a parent's popularity is in a nickname. In one of the photographs of their wedding day, my dad has his arm around one of their friends. My mum isn't wearing a wedding dress, and my dad, though wearing a smartish suit, isn't dressed up to the nines either. 'I didn't fancy a big wedding dress,' my mum said. 'Too corny! And we didn't have the money to hire a big fancy dress anyway. And I didn't want to wear white, what a cliché! Everyone wore white. I wore a yellow nylon flouncy dress with a narrow black belt and a full skirt. I had to pay it up, fifty bob a week.'

My mum joined the Communist Party in New Zealand at the same time as my dad. She always liked pointing out that her Maori friend Tam took them to their first meeting. Years later, back in Scotland, my dad gave up his work as a draughtsman in 1965 and started working as the Glasgow Secretary for the Communist Party when the Party offices were at 57 Miller Street. 'We'd have been a lot better off if he'd stuck to being a draughtsman and not worked full time for the Party. Still, he had to follow his passion.' My mum nearly got sacked from her job in her office at the box-making factory in New Zealand when she tried to get the other workers to sign a petition for Paul Robeson, the African-American singer and actor, to re-release his passport.

Just before their marriage in Christchurch, my mum's parents emigrated to New Zealand to join them. My mum was their only child; my dad too was an only child. I never had any cousins. I used to long for cousins and also wonder if they would have treated me and my brother, who is also adopted, exactly like cousins, or not. My mum's parents stayed in New Zealand for the next twenty-six years, missing Scotland and intensifying themselves abroad. When my gran returned, her Fife accent had become so broad, such a mixture of Lochgelly and nostalgia, that her old friends had difficulty understanding *her*! She was like a woman on a shortbread tin come to life; her Scottishness had become, all those miles away, the thing she valued about herself the most. There was a quaintness and kitschness to it; the years away had offered up a way of explaining herself that wasn't exactly truthful. Scotland the brave was a romantic place in her head: mist and battles, and misty battles. We used to roll up copies of the *Sunday Post*, containing Dudley Watkins's cartoons of oor Wullie and the Broons, and send them to my gran, who in turn rolled up copies of the *Christchurch Weekly* and sent them to us. I liked the rolled-up newspapers rolling in from abroad, and the idea that other people's news was different to ours. (We don't get that any more except perhaps from local papers in more remote areas. Recently in Ullapool on holiday, my dad was lost reading the Highland and Island local paper. 'Christ, it's fascinating. It's a whole different world.')

My mum and dad returned to Scotland after spending their first years of married life in New Zealand, much to the distress of my grandparents who had emigrated to join them there. By this time they desperately wanted children. They tried and tried but had no luck. This was in the days before IVF. They had tests done and still no luck. Eventually, it was my dad who suggested they might try adoption. My dad came up with many of the best ideas: a rucksack rather than a wedding ring, and adopted children rather a childless marriage. It took ages – my mum said five years – before they found an adoption agency that would accept them despite their politics. (I've realized it couldn't have been five years because they adopted my brother in 1959. It must have felt like five years.) In those days, the late fifties, adoption agencies were mostly run by religious organizations. There was the Glasgow Social Services, who wanted to know how often my parents went to church and how close they lived to a church. My parents wouldn't lie about this. 'There was that woman who said, "Just put anything down on the form, gloss over it." She was aff her heid!' my dad says, indignant. '"Just say you attend a weekly service, that'll be fine."'

'Why would we lie about something like that?' my mum says. 'Supposing we says, right we go to church three times a week and then they check up on us, and find we're lying? What then? Do they take the kid from us? When we first got Maxwell and you, we had to have you for two years before it was official. At any point, *at any point*, during that time, they could have come and took you away from us. And in those days the birth mother was allowed to change her mind within a six-month period.'

'Maybe she could see you were good people and was just trying to help you?' I say.

'Oh come on,' my mum says. 'What kind of help is that?'

'Maybe she wasn't used to people being so honest. You could have ended up not getting any child.'

'We couldn't lie, could we, John?' my mum says. My dad shakes his head angrily, the memory of it all annoys him. It all seems so wrong. 'Lie about how often you go to church, Christ, it's no real so it's no!'

'Well, I'm glad you didn't lie,' I say because suddenly, for the first time after all these years, after hearing the story several times, it occurs to me that had they lied, they would have been passed as eligible adoptive parents sooner, and would have adopted different children altogether. Not my brother. Not me. The thought that I might not have had them, Helen and John Kay, as my parents upsets me. So much was down to chance and timing. 'If you'd stayed in New Zealand,' I say, to make myself go down this horrible road further, 'you would have adopted different children.' My mum nods. 'I wonder what they would have been like?' She nods again. 'Maybe you'd have adopted Maori children?'

'Maybe,' my mum says, not much interested in this game of *what ifs*. 'It's all a lottery,' she says. 'It's all pure luck.'

After my parents finally got accepted by the Scottish Adoption Agency, and found a lovely woman who they felt was on their side, they went to a meeting where they were asked more questions. On the way out of this meeting, my mum remarked, and it was an almost casual, throw-away remark, 'By the way, we don't mind what colour the child is.' And the woman said, 'Really? Well, in that case we have a boy in the orphanage; we could let you see him today.' And if my mum hadn't thought to say that, just as she was leaving, my brother might have remained in the orphanage for the rest of his life, and so might have I, because having one 'coloured child' they decided to adopt another, to keep him company, which was forward-thinking, I see now looking back, for the sixties. 'To think they didn't even think to mention Maxie to us,' my mum says, still outraged at this, 'that he wasn't even thought of as a baby.'

'The day we visited Maxwell, in the orphanage, there were several other children we could have adopted as well,' my dad says.

'Really? You would have liked more?'

'Christ, yes,' my dad says. 'We shouldn't have worried so much about no being able to afford them. We could have given a home to two more at least. Remember that wee boy with the very dark eyes and hair,' my dad says. 'He just looked at us with these big brown eyes.' My dad's old blue eyes don't so much fill with tears as with a watery fluid that comes with age; thoughts that move him fill his eyes a little, as if his memory is a flooded place now, with things floating: children that needed homes, children he could have given a home to, children afloat on boards, like images of children flooded in New Orleans. The images all seem to mix together now, and it's as if my dad, being the good and kind man that he is, asks himself repeatedly if he made the right choices, if he did enough.

'We couldn't have had any more!' my mum says, impatiently. 'We couldn't afford them!'

'We could have always squeezed another in. Other people managed it!'

'You weren't even here most of the time. You were always out doing things for the Party. I couldn't have managed four on my own with you out every night till eleven.' My dad gives my mum a look as if she's hit below the belt, and used dirty tactics. I must have given her one too, because she looks at me and says, 'He wasn't around. You remember that! I was practically a single parent!' I know this is true, but I prefer the other truth for the moment; it too has something true about it that I've never heard before, the idea that my dad would have liked to have been a dad to four children, that he has somewhere in his head an idealistic idea of the kind of dad he would have liked to be – father to a gang of four, out in the Lost Glen, climbing the hills together.

My parents took my brother home on the 18th of September 1959. They always remember the day they got him home because it was the same day as the Auchengeich Colliery disaster, when forty-eight men lost their lives. 'It was terrible. Just dreadful! And when the anniversary of that came round, I always remembered that was the day we got our Maxwell home.' My mum's father had been a miner from Lochgelly and had twice been buried alive down the pits, and twice survived, and she had grown up in a house full of miners. She remembered being offered a penny for washing the backs of her mining uncles when they sat in the steel tub bath, and how by the weekend they would also ask for their penny back to go dancing. She remembers the coal-filthy thick oilskins.

Shortly after the day they brought my brother home, a minister arrived at my parents' door. ' "I've heard that you've done a kind act and adopted *a coloured child*," he says to me,' my mum said. ' "We at the Church just wanted to know if we could be of any assistance," as if he were thinking of you both as *noble savages*. I sent him packing,' my mum told me, 'I'll tell you what's savage, the Scottish Presbyterian Church!' I don't know if this really happened, the minister on the doorstep, or if it's apocryphal, but my mum used to insist that it did, though I also know that I have inherited, if inherited is the word, and perhaps it is, her gift for exaggeration. 'Did I tell you of the time that I was locked up in a church?' my mum says. 'Your father and I were both arrested at a protest against Polaris. Your dad was taken to the gaol in Dunoon, but then they ran out of space in the gaol, there were that many protesters, so they locked me and other women up in the Catholic Church. That's the most time I've ever spent in a church,' my mum said laughing. 'Mind you, I got out before your father. I remember being back at home and the policeman turning up at the door and saying, "Do you know your husband is in prison?" and me saying, "Aye, and I'm just out." Your grandmother was very judgemental about it all.

Well, she was very God-fearing. I remember your dad and I were both fined, ten pounds each, which was a *huge* amount then, and it wasn't fair, two from the one family.' My mum never got on that well with my other gran, my dad's mum. I remember her saying that the only good thing my gran had to say about her was that she was 'a neat walker'.

A couple of years after they adopted my brother, my mum had a call from the same woman at the Scottish Adoption Agency. 'There's a woman who has come down from the Highlands, and the father of the baby is from Nigeria. We thought we'd let you know since you told us you wanted another child the same colour.' So, months before my birth mother gave birth to me, my mum knew that she was going to have me. 'It was the closest I could get to giving birth myself,' she's told me often. 'I didn't know if I'd have a girl or a boy, if you'd be healthy or not, the kind of thing that no mother knows. It was a real experience. It felt real. I remember waiting and waiting for news of your birth and phoning up every day to find out if you'd been born yet. Finally, I was told you had been born, you were a girl, but you were not healthy. And they advised me to come in and pick another baby, because you weren't expected to live. The forceps had caused some brain damage, and also left a gash down your face. The brain damage still shows,' my mum said, laughing. I like hearing this fairytale; I've heard it often. My mum wouldn't pick another baby; she'd become attached to the idea of me in the months of ghost pregnancy, where she'd shadowed my birth mother in her own imagination, picturing, perhaps, her belly getting bigger and bigger. She already felt like I belonged to her. She visited every week, or every month, depending when she's telling the story, driving the forty miles from Glasgow to Edinburgh, with my dad, and she had to wear a mask, so as not to infect me, and got to pick me up and hold me. Perhaps this interest, this love, is what made me survive against the odds. The doctors were apparently amazed at my recovery.

Then after five months she was finally allowed to take me home. My brother was told they were going to collect his baby sister, and he was excited about it, my mum said. 'And protective from the word go. He'd guard that big navy Silver Cross pram, and if anybody peered in, he'd announce that you were his sister. We had to feed you a special diet – it *worked*! By Jesus, it *worked* all right! – porridge and extra vitamins, to build up your strength. A few weeks later, the woman from the Agency rang again saying your birth mother had requested a baby photograph.'

'Did she?' I asked.

My mum nodded. 'She did. So we propped you up in the back garden, that was before the grass had been sown and the back was mostly mud, and went to take a picture, but you went flying back. That was the first picture we took of you that one where you are flying back.

'And then we took another, better picture, and I put it in the post, but I never heard anything back. I know that they sent it on because she was reliable that woman, and kind. A while later I received a wee knitted yellow cardigan for you in the post that had been knitted by your birth mother.'

'You did?'

'I did,' she nods. 'I don't remember you ever telling me that before.'

'No? Probably just forgot. Maybe I've even made it up. Maybe I thought she should have knitted you something. You get all mixed up with what's the truth and what's not. I know she went back up to the Highlands. She lived with her grandmother. I imagined she'd been encouraged to have her baby adopted, put it that way. It wouldn't have been the norm in those days, a black man with a white woman. It must have been a hell of a lonely journey back to that wee Highland town of Nairn. I was told her address there was Ivy Cottage.'

When I was seventeen and my mum was the age I am now, we went on a wee holiday, just the two of us, staying at various B and Bs in the north of Scotland. We passed through Elgin and into Nairn. 'Why don't we try and find that Ivy Cottage, just to see,' my mum said, excitedly. 'We can do our Columbo.' We went into a red phone box and looked up the surname Fraser. We found so many Frasers it was staggering, Fraser the butcher, Fraser the baker, Fraser the plumber, but only one that lived at an Ivy Cottage. 'You hide behind the corner, in case they see you,' my mum said. Then she knocked at the door, and said she was looking for an Elizabeth Fraser, that she used to nurse with her. (She'd known that my mother was a nurse.) 'Whoever answered the door wasn't very friendly,' my mum told my dad when we got back to Glasgow.

'And no bloody wonder,' my dad said, angrily. 'That was irresponsible of you. What if it had been her? What might you have walked straight into? You don't know what kind of can of worms you might have been opening.'

My mum shrugged as if my dad's response bored her. 'We thought we were playing at being detectives,' my mum said, as far as she was concerned it'd all just been a bit of fun, and he was being a real stick in the mud.

'You're out of your mind!' my dad said. 'And having Jackie hide round the corner! Honestly, Ellen! Who knows what could have happened?'

'But there was definitely something she wasn't telling us,' my mum said. 'She knew an Elizabeth Fraser, that's for sure. She was hostile. Why should she be hostile? All I was doing was saying I used to work with an Elizabeth Fraser, nothing more.'

'You're a stranger on her doorstep. Naebody likes strangers on their doorsteps least of all folk with something to hide,' my dad said and hid behind his *Morning Star* in a fury. My mum rolled her eyes at me. I was her accomplice and her daughter. We had both wanted to find my mother just out of curiosity, we told ourselves. Neither of us had given proper thought to what might have happened next had my birth mother answered the door. My dad was right, we'd acted irresponsibly, it was a trail we were on, but we hadn't seriously considered where it might have ended.

I think that my mum was interested in tracking my birth mother down in the same way that I was a little later in my life when I did the whole thing for real. For her, she wanted to see the person she had imagined, the one who had gifted her me. I think my mum liked the idea of turning up on a stranger's doorstep and the stranger turning out to be somebody related to my birth mother who could have put us in the right direction. Then we could have followed the star through the day and night and turned up on another doorstep, and might have been taken in, and welcomed, and fed and watered.

My mum knew that had she ever been lucky enough to fall pregnant, nothing would have ever persuaded her to give her baby up for adoption. There was always something mysterious in the story of our adoption, mysterious to my mum, something made up about it. And then again other people made up stories too about us. Around the time when my mum and dad got me from Elsie Inglis Hospital in Edinburgh, they had a Communist Party member staying with them from Uganda. 'I think the neighbours all thought I'd had an affair,' my mum said, relishing this other self. And then shortly after they'd got me back from the hospital they had a party in our house, a Party social, and another comrade from Nigeria was staying over. Margaret Akinwuma, whose brother was Secretary for the Nigerian Peace Committee. She was bobbing me on her lap and everyone assumed I belonged to her. Margaret thought it was funny. 'And then whenever I went out with you in the pram and people looked in, they never knew what to say, so they'd often say, "She looks a lot like you."'

People still do tell me that I look like my mum, which is maybe true. Perhaps after years of unconsciously copying her physical mannerisms and gestures, I've grown to look like her. Or perhaps, by some fluke, we just do.

We often held parties in our house, Party socials and parties for neighbours and friends. I loved getting the buffet ready for these occasions with my mum. I liked copying the way she did things. We'd cut the tomatoes in zigzag style, put little squares of cheese on sticks with chunks of pineapple or pickled onions, roll sliced ham, cut sausage rolls in half, and sometimes, if we were being very adventurous, we'd make our own coleslaw. (I remember the day my mum first discovered coleslaw. She came back from the shops all excited, and said, 'You'll never guess what I've discovered?' 'What?' I said. 'This new amazing thing called coleslaw.') We'd put out little bowls full of beetroot balls or slices of cucumber, or bowls of crisps, and assemble everything so that it looked pretty and colourful. 'There,' my mum would say with satisfaction, 'that looks pretty.' Then the people would arrive and the drinks would start to flow and soon the singing would start too, and before long, my dad would be taking to the floor singing his favourites: 'St James Infirmary Blues', 'Well Alright OK You Win', a Joe Williams song that I grew into singing with him, even though I'm tone deaf. *I'll do anything you want, anything you wa-aaaant me to. Sing hey bob a loo loo. Hey bob a loo loo . . .* Or Cole Porter's 'Brush up Your Shakespeare': *The girls today in society, Go for classical poetry, so to win their hearts one must quote with ease, Aeschylus and Euripides. But the poet of them all, Who will start 'em simply raving, is the poet people call, the bard of Stratford-on-Avon.* Or more unusual songs like 'The Wilds of Croftamie': *Far away in the hills of Croftamie, where the white man fears to tread.* And Alec Clark would sing 'Ae Fon Kiss', and Anna Ashton would sing 'John Anderson my jo', and Peter Morton would sing, and Kenny Haldane would sing, and I would feel happy, gloriously happy, surrounded by people who had their songs with them. All of my happiest memories are about people singing to me: Ali singing 'Maxwellton Braes are Bonny' in her sweet Highland voice, Nick singing 'Stormy Weather' in his soaring, tender voice; Ella, Carol Ann's daughter, singing 'Every time We Say Goodbye' in her pure and jazzy fourteen-year-old voice.

'One singer, one song,' somebody would shout, back then, and it was somebody else's turn. People danced up and down our small living-room floor, acting their songs out. My dad had an imaginary brush to accompany his rendition of 'Brush up Your Shakespeare'. The Party was a party, a rave, but also a party, a group of like-minded people who enjoyed each other's company and shared similar values. Years later, there were divisions amongst them about which directions the Party should take. But in my childhood at least the Party seemed to be like an extended family. Because we had very little money, the Party butcher made us a packet of meat on a Saturday for a fiver that would last us the week. It contained four steaks – 'four steaks, the generosity!' my dad would enthuse – four square sausages, the kind of sausage my gran missed when she was in New Zealand. Only the Scottish would think to make a sausage square, my dad said. Four rashers of bacon, 'Look at that, hardly any fat on it!' Four slices of black pudding. Four slices of fruit pudding. Half a dozen eggs. 'No bad for a fiver, even for them days.' The Party carpenter would fit bookshelves for next to nothing. When the plumbing went in the bathroom, the Party plumber came and fixed it for next to nothing too.

Every so often my mum and dad qualified for a free Party holiday. They went to Moscow, Leningrad, Petersburg. The year they went off to Russia, they left my brother and me with comrades Jack and Anna Ashton for three weeks. Jack and Anna couldn't have us all the time, so they took us to another comrade, who we'd never met, who lived in a wee cottage on the outskirts of Edinburgh, at the end of a very overgrown garden. I was seven; Maxie was nine. The wee man had baked a huge gooseberry pie. I've never tasted another like it. The juice from the gooseberries was oozing out of a hole in the middle. The wee man had peculiar habits. He would pee into a milk bottle at night, and in the morning the bottle would be half full of his pee, an intense orangey yellow. I remember seeing the bottle on a shelf in his kitchen, and staring at the colour for ages, half appalled, half fascinated. Then he would beat up a raw egg for his breakfast, add a little of the piss, 'to gie it the right consistency', and half a pint of milk, transfer the mixture to a glass and knock it back in one. 'Never been sick a day in my life,' the old man said. I couldn't wait for my parents to return from Russia.

This was my mum's second visit to Russia. She had been once before for a World Youth Congress in 1958, before she got my brother. 'You had to be under thirty to go, so your dad missed out. From Scotland, Calum Kennedy the number-one folk singer of the era went, and Robin Hall and Jimmie MacGregor, the folk-singing duo, went, people from all backgrounds went including the Bow Hill Pipe Band who led the whole British contingent.' My mum travelled through Europe on a train, and at every stop, people from all over the world got on. She was in her element: Jamaicans, Poles, Nigerians, Spanish, Cubans. She had the journey of her life. At Warsaw, they changed trains and my mum was asked to organize where everyone should sleep on the new train and she forgot to include herself so she had to share a sleeping compartment with two Indian men, who were mortified. Between them they made elaborate arrangements about how to get undressed without them seeing my mum or her seeing them.

Every time I hear of that epic journey, of those young people meeting on a train heading for Moscow, I think of it as a story that leads to my brother and me; in an

33

imaginary way, the train stopped at us. We could have been picked up en route. We could have been from anywhere in the world. All my parents knew about my brother's original family was that his grandfather was said to have come off a boat and landed in Leith. Nobody knew from where and my mum often amused herself by thinking about all the countries my brother could possibly have come from, and even, sometimes, all the continents: somewhere in Africa maybe, or the Caribbean or maybe even Latin America. The mystery of her own children was as compelling, for my mum, as DNA, as genetically inherited traits or features. I remember her often saying to me throughout my childhood, 'Our Maxie is an enigma to me.' She didn't just mean where he came from; she also meant his character and personality. The other thing she liked to say was, 'You can choose your friends, but you can't choose your family.' She'd usually say this with reference to some friend or another having difficulty with some member of her family. But the thing that used to strike me about that cliché was that in my mum's case it wasn't true: she had chosen her family.

1971

I am wearing a red trouser suit. The trousers are flared. I'm wearing turquoise crinkly leather platform shoes. My hair is as big as Angela Davis' hair. I have a poster of her on my bedroom wall. It says FREE ANGELA DAVIS. Today, I'm attending a big rally for the UCS. The UCS stands for Upper Clyde Shipbuilders. They are having a work-in instead of a strike. My dad says that Uncle Jimmy has told the workers, No Hooliganism, no Vandalism and no Bevvying. My Uncle Jimmy is speaking at the rally. My dad is rushing around. Everyone knows me because everyone knows my dad. I feel quite famous. Jack Ashton stops to say hello to me. He says, Nice colour, comrade, admiring my trouser suit. I haven't been called comrade before. I quite like it. It stays in my head and I say it to myself in the mirror, looking at my red trouser suit; nice colour, comrade.

The McClennan Galleries is the same place where the Morning Star Bazaar is held every Christmas. I love the bazaar. My brother works the candyfloss machine, and there's lots of interesting things to buy with my pocket money.

The next interesting thing after the Morning Star Bazaar, apart from Christmas, is the Burns Supper. My dad will do the immortal memory and Maisie Hill will be brilliant and scary addressing the Haggis. Then it's May Day when we'll all go to Jessie Clark's house for her brilliant food and I'll play in her huge back garden that has lots of apple trees after we've listened to the brass band in Queen's Park. Then after May Day, it's the Miners' Gala in Edinburgh. We'll all march down the Royal Mile. At the bottom of the Royal Mile the old people sitting in wheelchairs and ordinary chairs will be out in the sun to watch the procession going by. We are the procession. They'll be watching us going by.

My friend Margaret says to me that a lot of people in the Party admire my parents for adopting my brother and me, and that we should be grateful. When I tell my mum this, she's furious. She says Never Ever let Anyone tell You YOU should be grateful! WE are the ones who are Grateful!

Uncle Jimmy is handsome with dark wavy hair. Everyone gets very worked up when he speaks. My dad says he's got political savvy. He says Angela Davis is a political heroine. I'd like to be a political heroine. I wonder if I'd still wear a red trouser suit if I grew up into a political heroine.

Fantasy Africa

In my imaginary childish drawing, my birth father is a tall, handsome black man with large hands and dark life lines and a broad smile. He is a rich dark colour, a melting darkness, warm and endless like the dark of sleep. He has broad features, a wide nose, high spread cheeks, wide as the span of a small bird's wing, and a laughing smile. When I trace round the edges of the bold picture-book picture, he becomes a bit fuzzier, a bit less whole. He has black curly hair, but I can't quite see its texture, I can't imagine the smallness of the curls. His eyes are black and dark and I can't read them. I don't know this man. I have never met him yet. I like making him up now and again, like children make up stories, or draw bright pictures. He is proud; he is clever; he is noble. Like the young Sidney Poitier or Nelson Mandela or Martin Luther King or Cassius Clay – the only real images of black men I have at my disposal – I imagine my father possesses great dignity, stature. (Dignity oddly enough seems to come with height; the dignified are always tall in the imagination. A small person has to scrabble a bit to acquire dignity!) Yes, my father, a tall handsome black man, a good black man who would give his goodness *for the world* as all good black men have to.

I was never told much about my father because my parents were never told much. Adopted people were told hardly anything then, not like today when children are given whole family books, photographs, information and in some instances are encouraged, through open adoptions, to keep in touch with their birth parents. It is an intriguing concept but I always wonder how can a child live in two worlds with only one life?

I was told two things, really. One: he studied agriculture at the University of Aberdeen; two: he was from Nigeria. Nigeria was a country in West Africa and West Africa was very far away from Glasgow. Africa itself could only ever be imagined in the way that I imagined my father, with bright picture-book colours and bold outlines. Part of me came from Africa, part of me was foreign to myself, strange to myself since I had never been to the *dark continent* and could only really have it burning away, hot and dusty, in my mind. It is not so much that being black in a white country means that people don't accept you as, say, Scottish; it is that being black in a white country makes you a stranger to yourself. It is not the foreigner without; it is the foreigner within that is interesting. Every time somebody in your own country asks you where you are from; every time you indignantly reply, 'I'm from here,' you are subconsciously caught up in asking that question again and again of yourself, particularly when you are a child. Children have an intense need to belong

38

and anything that marks them out as different from all the other children will then form a straggly queue of uneasy, queasy questions in their head.

What did we learn about Africa in school? Not a lot – but I never relished *Africa* coming up *in any way at all* and always took the continent very personally because my classmates would look at me whenever *Africa* was mentioned (hardly ever individual countries, just a whole mass as if it was one country), sneakily turning round to stare and pull faces. African people lived in mud huts in appalling poverty, wore grass skirts and tribal make-up, had strange cuts in their faces to indicate their tribes, were primitive, unsophisticated. Something about sex was hinted at but not spoken. (Big penises, whisper, whisper.) Africans could dance; they had natural rhythm. There was jungle out there in Africa – jungle and bush, lions and elephants. There were African elephants which had different ears from Indian elephants. It was hot in Africa. The people were very dark. The people were wild savages. When they were born they were put into an oven to make them darker so that their skin did not burn in the sun. There were bongo drums in Africa, witch doctors and strange wild dances, lots of chanting and humming and squealing. Superstition was big in Africa. African people were not logical thinkers. African people were irrational, hot-tempered. African people were more like stories and myths than rational, logical human beings.

When Christianity arrived in Africa, according to this

version, things looked up, but it was still a terrible problem getting the people to turn their back on voodoo and superstition and the like. The African people were so into the chiefs' business and the tribes and the ancient traditions of the homelands that there were big problems dragging them, screaming and chanting and dancing, into the twentieth century. Where did it all come from? Of course those images and stereotypes have changed over the last forty years but some of them persist and bubble underneath the foundations of the society we live in now. Black people are still seen in a rather unsophisticated way, good or bad, coconuts or dropouts, still categorized, and still not afforded the same basic right as white people – to be seen as a whole person. In many ways, we still live in a rather primitive racist society.

It is important to think about it, especially when you are a black person yourself and still have to struggle to remove the assumptions and stereotypes that nibble at your own brain. 'Every colonized people . . . every people in whose soul an inferiority complex has been created by the death and burial of its local cultural originality – finds itself face to face with the language of the civilizing nation . . . The colonized is elevated above his jungle status in proportion to his adoption of the mother country's cultural standards. He becomes whiter as he renounces his blackness, his jungle,' Franz Fanon said in a seminal book, *Black Skin, White Masks*. I remember reading Fanon in my early twenties, electrified; reading changed the mirror that I held up to myself. I remember the excitement of coming across writers like Audre Lorde, Alice Walker, Toni Morrison, Ralph Ellison. All of those writers changed my racial awareness; reading them changed my life.

When I traced the outline of my imaginary father, only certain parts of his face would be distinct at any given moment. Not the entire face. It was a bit like when you do a rubbing from a coin, one part emerges sooner than the other and one part is always more detailed. One minute I could see his lips clearly, his mouth, thick lips, like my own, a square-shaped face, like my own. It is strange how little the imagination needs to form a picture; it needs less than a fire to get it started. It needs no kindling, firelighters, no newspapers rolled up thinly, no logs, coal or peat. All the imagination needs is the spark of this with the rub of that. It needs a tiny seed; before you know where you are there's a huge rubber plant in your living room swallowing all of the air. Two things about my father: he studied agriculture and he came from Nigeria. My mum obviously didn't need much either. And for most of my childhood, my mum's sparkling imagination lit mine. I often wonder whether or not I'd have been that interested in being adopted if my mum hadn't been so fascinated by it all.

'Maybe your father was an African chief,' my mother used to say, and, 'Maybe you are an African princess.' I liked that. In my imaginary princess picture, I am wearing a traditional African dress, purples and oranges and yellows. 'Maybe you will own land,' my mother said.

I liked that too. I pictured the plots of my land in the African landscape of my imagination. It was flat land, not like the Highlands of Scotland. The earth was dark and rich. There was a red-dust road. I couldn't really get much further than that.

'*Betrothed*,' she told me, 'your father met your mother in the Highlands of Scotland and they fell in love. He was from Nigeria – look, here it is in the atlas – and she was from the Highlands – look, here's where she was from, Nairn. They were madly in love and they made you, but he was *betrothed* and had to return to Nigeria to marry a woman he maybe had never even met. They do that there, you know. Hard, Jackie, must have been hard.' My mum rolled the word *betrothed* round on her tongue like an old-fashioned sweetie from an old-fashioned sweetie shop, a cinnamon ball or a soor ploom or a sherbet lemon. *Betrothed*. The word itself had a sweet romantic flavour, something exotic about it. Something other-worldly. You could never imagine somebody from Ballachulish or Auchtermuchty getting *betrothed*. Betrothed, all the way across the ocean, *th, sh, th, sssssssshhhhh* in West Africa, in Nigeria, in some part there where they still had old ways, old ways of the people. That was a clash, an academic student who was also *betrothed*. 'Although your father loved your mother he would have had to abandon her, while she was pregnant, imagine, Jackie, and return to Nigeria to this woman he wasn't in love with like he was in love with your mother. It's a whole different ball game out there. Your father would have been doing the

42

honourable thing.' I liked this story too; this story of betrothal which was also perhaps a story of betrayal.

What did we have to go on, me and my mum when we made things up? Not a whole lot – agriculture – or was it forestry? And Nigeria. It is what the imagination feasts off, the bone, not the meat, the bits that are left behind. The less you are given the more you can make up. At the time I believed my mum and she possibly believed it herself in that way that people do; once you make a story up, it is hard not to believe it yourself. We all do that. We never know where the truth ends and the story starts and in a way it doesn't matter. It shouldn't matter who my birth father really is, who my birth mother really is. It shouldn't matter a bit. It shouldn't matter because I know my parents who brought me up. I know John and Helen Kay; I know who they are.

I wonder if my mum gave us these stories because she thought they compensated for being given up for adoption. There were the stories of my original parents having no choice, and the stories of my mum and dad having choice. 'We *chose* you; you are special. Other people had to take what they got, but we *chose* you.' It was *circumstances* that prevented my mother marrying my father; it was *circumstances* that sent him back to Nigeria; it was *circumstances* that made it impossible for my mother to keep me on her own. It wasn't done then, in the sixties. Illegitimacy was scandalous. Times have changed. 'You have to understand!' My mum did. She understood *circumstances* and she wanted me to understand them too. And I did. I will always be thankful to my mum for giving me that way of seeing, for stopping me from seeing myself as somebody who was rejected. Instead I saw myself as somebody who had been chosen. And I felt huge empathy for both of my birth parents, thwarted in their love, a love that couldn't properly be understood at that time, between a black Nigerian man and a white Highland girl. My mum told me that my mother had been forced to give me up because of racism in the Highlands. My birth mother, according to my mum, had been brought up by her grandmother in the Highlands and her grandmother had disapproved of her being with a black man and had sent my mother down to Edinburgh to have me, sent her to one of those appalling and judgemental mother-and-baby homes. 'Just imagine that!' I did. I imagined my birth mother pregnant with me and having to mop floors and clean toilets on her own, away from her family in the Highlands, carrying a baby she could not keep. It was a heartbreaking story and it was mine. In a way my mum and I loved it, the story of me. It was a big bond, the story.

My mum's imagination is vivid and her language is bright. My brother's story of adoption and mine were the two first big real stories I heard, and we found both stories fascinating: stories of black men coming off boats, stories of black blood (when my brother was adopted my mum told us that they had done tests on him in Edinburgh to see if he had any 'negro blood' because they couldn't explain his colour. Then my mum said that my brother

44

was what was known as a '*throwback*'). Stories of family trees and boats and origins and Nigeria and goodness knows where for my brother, somewhere off the coast of somewhere else, far away, stories of cultures so totally, so utterly different from kitsch Scottish culture, Burns suppers and haggis, shortbread and square sausage, Irn Bru, and kilts.

Perhaps for my mum there was something exotic and special about her two children who arrived with their stories in their Moses baskets. My mum used to say on my birthday every year I can remember, 'Somewhere out there is a woman who is thinking, "That child I had will be eight today, nine today . . ."' This was a sad but lovely idea and my mum and I both thought about my other mother with compassion. My mum was crediting this other mother with exactly her own sensibility, her sensitivity, her outlook. Not for a single second was my mum thinking that there might be another mother somewhere who never bothered to think about me on my birthday. My mum was not capable of conjuring up a mother for me who didn't feel regret, or longing, or loss.

My mum all those years ago sensed a child who had been adopted was also a child who could feel terribly hurt. And no matter how much she loved me, no matter how much my dad loved me, there is still a windy place right at the core of my heart. The windy place is like Wuthering Heights, out on open moors, rugged and wild and free and lonely. The wind rages and batters at the trees. I struggle against the windy place. I sometimes even forget it. But

45

there it is. I am partly defeated by it. You think adoption is a story which has an end. But the point about it is that it has no end. It keeps changing its ending.

It infuriates me that this windy place exists at all. It shouldn't. I have been incredibly lucky. I have two parents who love me. I have very close and good friends. I have a wonderful and perceptive son, Matthew. I have a lovely, warm-hearted and kind lover. I am lucky. I am blessed. And yet still, sometimes, in my dark hours, there is this feeling that I am alone. And I can't shake it. There's this ghostly something. I am only alone in the way that everybody is alone. And yet it seems that the bundle of child that is wrapped up in the ghostly shawl of adoption does have another layer of aloneness wrapped up in there.

There are essentially two kinds of adopted people: the ones who never trace, who never want to, are not interested, or who are frightened of hurting their adoptive parents' feelings; and the ones who want to trace, who are curious about their origins, who think that in tracing their original parents they will understand themselves better. In a way I would have loved to have been one of the ones who wasn't bothered, who had never set the ball rolling and who wasn't now in the position of the ball rolling all the way to the bottom of the hill. *You and me, baby, all the way to the end of the line.* The end of the line is where you finally realize that the imagination was not so bad at all. But in another way I can't understand the lack of curiosity. Those people who are given various little snips of information about themselves and deliberately choose to take it no further are a mystery to me. Are they cowards? Or are they quite sensible?

Others, like me, turn and walk back up the road to their past in search of themselves. Why do people my age, forty-odd, go off and trace their birth parents? Surely it is too late by then? Why do we even want to know; surely we know ourselves by now? Why should we have any curiosity, never mind the blazing burning curiosity, the all-consuming insatiable appetite for self-knowledge that some of us feel? If we think of ourselves as puzzles, and our birth parents are part of that puzzle, do we think that finding our parents will answer the puzzle? Surely we are not so naive?

The jigsaw can never, ever be completed. There will always be missing pieces, or the pieces will be too large and clumsy to fit into the delicate puzzle. The search is often disappointing because it is a false search. You cannot find yourself in two strangers who happen to share your genes. You are made already, though you don't properly know it, you are made up from a mixture of myth and gene. You are part fable, part porridge. Finding a strange, nervous, Mormon mother and finding a crazed, ranting, Born-Again father does not explain me. At least I hope not! *Please, God, thank you, God.* (But right enough I do have a tendency to rant on about things and I do like to coerce people into seeing my point of view – *Help!*) I have found them both now. But I have not found myself. I had already found myself. I already knew who I was, I think. Or did I?

I have my father's hands and feet. I have my mother's mouth. I have my father's forehead and jaw. I have my mother's hair. I have my father's sense of humour, gift of the gab. I have my mother's sensitivity. What does it matter? And why is it interesting at all? Is it interesting? I met my birth father for the very first time on a Sunday, a Sunday in Nigeria with Jonathan. For some people, tracing turns out to be a wonderful experience, a bit like an exhilarating love affair. Some people describe the feeling of meeting a birth parent for the first time as akin to being in love. For others it is pretty disastrous. But no matter whether the experience is positive or negative – it churns you up. It turns your life upside down. It is something that should not be done lightly. You wouldn't imagine such an innocent activity, tracing, sketching over something that had already been sketched over before, could be so life-changing.

1976

I've got a boyfriend from Nigeria called Femi. He's tall and very good looking. My mum wants to meet him so I bring him home. I walk the long way from the bus stop up Brackenbrae Road, past the Fort Theatre because I don't want everyone seeing me with Femi at Bishopbriggs Cross, and I'm afraid people might call him names. But also I'm a bit embarrassed. And I'm embarrassed about being embarrassed.

The feeling reminds me of a time when I was a wee girl, five or six. My grandmother had sent me a black doll, a Maori doll from New Zealand. She was huge, with orange eyes, a grass skirt and a feather top. She was a warm dark brown colour and had dark black hair. I called her Niari, which I was told was a Maori name. I was walking her down my street in her pram when a bigger girl stopped and looked in. She said, Just cos you're a darkie doesn't mean you have to have a darkie doll.

I took Niari home and I locked her in the airing cupboard. I locked her in with the warm sheets and towels and spare blankets. Every so often I'd feel very guilty and get her out and hug her. I'd explain the whole situation to her. I'm sorry, Niari, I'd say. Mummy is sorry. I'd ask her if she was lonely.

I feel as if people will look at me more because I'm with

Femi. My parents like Femi. They ask him if he's feeling the cold in Glasgow, and he says yes, he is and laughs. The winter is very cold here. My dad gives him a thick winter coat that he doesn't wear any more. Femi's delighted with it. We have scones and blackcurrant jam and mugs of tea. I take my tea the same way as my grandfather, with no milk in it. On the way back to the bus stop, I walk Femi the short way round through the Park and down to the Cross. We walk hand in hand. His hands remind me of the hands of a black man who stayed at my house when I was four. He was the first black man I ever saw in my life. I found him entrancing. He had dark life lines and I liked tracing the dark life lines on his long hands.

Manchester

Early in May 2003, I attended a conference where I met a French academic. Martine Spensky told me that she had traced her birth father, an Argentinian Jew from Russian parents, through Google, and that if my birth father was an academic, he should be easy to find. 'Just one article and he'll be on the net,' she said. I was amazed that it had never occurred to me to Google my father! Over the years I'd thought of getting in touch with Aberdeen University's student records. I'd thought of writing to the Nigerian Embassy, who supported the students who came to Scotland in the sixties. I'd been told by various Nigerian friends that, with a surname, he should be easy enough to trace; surnames give you a rough idea of the part of Nigeria people are from.

Years earlier, I'd been on a night train from London to Manchester after having done a poetry gig. (It's funny how we poets call readings gigs, really sad and pathetic, just to pretend we are pop stars. We meet each other on the road and say, 'Done any good gigs recently?' 'Yes, Milton Keynes Central Library.') A black man, sitting opposite me, looked at my face and said suddenly, 'I bet you are an

Igbo. Igbo – definitely!' It was such a striking experience that I wrote a poem about it.

I discovered the man on the train was right. My father was an Igbo. I came back from the conference and told my partner what the French academic had said. I then put my father's name into Google and within seconds up popped Pop! The speed was shocking. Completely different to the slow and patient way that I had found my mother, trailing though old records of marriages and births in New Register House, the house that keeps records in Edinburgh. There he was and there was a photograph of him, and an article about his work on trees. It was astonishing. There I was tracing my family tree only to discover a tree-specialist father; if I put it in a novel, no one would believe me. The article on the Internet had a phone number. My partner and I decided to ring right away. Carol Ann said she would talk to him first. The time in Nigeria is the same as the time in the UK. We called and a voice said the Professor wasn't in, but we should call back in half an hour. Half an hour later, Carol Ann rang back and said, 'Hello, is that Professor O? My name is Professor Duffy, I teach at Manchester University. I understand you went to Aberdeen?' My father obviously confirmed this. 'I'm wondering if you knew an Elizabeth Fraser?' 'You did?' Carol Ann nodded excitedly to me. 'Well, you might know that she had a baby over forty years ago? The baby was called Joy? You asked for her to be called Joy? Well, she is now called Jackie. She is a good friend of mine. Where is she? She is standing right next to me!'

'Put her on the phone,' my father says to Carol Ann. 'Put her on the phone!'

She hands the phone to me. 'He wants to talk to you.' And so I speak to my father for the first time.

'How are you?' he says. I can hardly breathe with excitement. I can't believe it. My father was just a click of the mouse and a phone call away, and half an hour after entering his name into the search engine I'm talking to him on the telephone. And he is in Nigeria. I tell him I'm coming to Nigeria and would very much like to meet him. 'Why are you coming to Nigeria?' he says, sounding anxious.

'I'm coming to do some work. I'm a writer. I'm going to be in Abuja, Kano and Lagos.'

'I see. I see. Let me think about this,' he says. I ask him for an email address so that I can write to him and he gives me it. He asks me if I believe in God. He says, 'God has intended for us to be in touch at this stage in my life.' I say I believe in good things, peace on earth, and good-will to my fellow human beings. 'But God?' he presses. 'Do you believe in God?'

'Well, maybe that is for a longer conversation,' I say nervously. We talk a little longer. He says that he might not be my father, and how am I absolutely certain, that a lot of women in those days were busy enjoying themselves. 'My birth mother was pretty certain it is you,' I say to him, a little flabbergasted at this, privately thinking that I must write to my birth mother and double check. I don't want to go all the way to Nigeria to meet the wrong man.

He wishes me well, and says he is happy to have heard from me and that he will write and send some photographs. He says, 'God bless you, my dear,' before he hangs up. I can barely take it in. I feel in shock. I sit down and write my first email to my father.

Date: 13 May 2003 16:29

Dear Jonathan,

It was very exciting to talk with you this morning. I feel glad to have found you. I will be coming to Nigeria later this year and hope to meet you then. I'll be visiting Abuja, Kano and Lagos. Are you near any of these places? Where do you live? I traced my birth mother some years ago and she told me your name and that you'd met at Aberdeen. Funnily enough I am going to Aberdeen this weekend to read my poetry at the university.

I have a son who is fourteen years old, Matthew, and is very tall and bright. I make my living writing poetry. I don't want to overload you with too many details. It would be lovely to hear a bit more about you and your interests and your family. I was pleased to hear of your work with trees since I have always loved trees. It's wonderful that you've done so much for them. I was brought up in Glasgow with a very loving and kind Scottish couple who also adopted a boy, my brother. When my adoptive mum

*heard I would be going to Nigeria in the autumn,
she asked if I might try and find you. She is as
curious as I am. If you have any photographs of
yourself, I would love to have them. You might email
them to me or post them to me.*

*I'd also be very interested in seeing a photo of your
parents and hearing a little about them.*

*I hope to hear from you soon. In the meantime,
every good wish and love,*

Jackie xxxx

15/5/03

Dear Jackie,

*Thank you so much for your mail, soon after our
first ever telephone conversation and I share the
sentiments expressed. When and how long would
you be at Abuja, Kano and Lagos respectively?
I have a spiritual urge to meet you at Abuja.*

*My professional interests are plant taxonomy,
ethnobotany, ethnomedicine, environmental
conservation and beautification, domestication
of fruit trees etc.*

*I spend a great deal of time on evangelism,
preaching, healing etc. I am a licensed Lay Reader
of Anglican Church and Chapter President of Full*

Gospel Business Men's Fellowship International.
God has planned for us to be in contact at this stage
of my career when I am a born again Christian
(see 2Cor 5:17) Read also Rom 3:23; Rom 10:9&10;
Jn 1:12; Jn 3:3–6 and Phil. 3:13. When we meet
we shall deliberate on the issue of new birth. I have
started praying for you and Mathew, Jer 29:11
applies to both of you. Amen. As I mentioned on the
phone, I have 4 children, 3 boys and 1 girl. They are
all established ie married with children except the
last boy. My parents were traders (on cloth and fish)
respectively, but they are dead in 1979 and 1989.
I shall send you my photographs by post. I am a
consultant. I am excited that you are a poet and
novelist. I thank God for your adoptive parents who
helped you to climb to such height.

Remain blessed,

Jonathan

Ps I have decided to send this by post since it could
not go by email for incomplete address or so!

1977

It is November and instead of having PE we have to have dancing lessons to practise for the school Christmas dance. We, the girls, are lined up on one side of the hall, and the boys are lined up on the other side, near the window. The teacher bellows, Boys, go and pick your dancing partner! And the boys charge across the hall. Each time I hope for a different outcome, but each time it is me, Yuk Lan, the Chinese girl, and Rhona, the girl with the bright red hair, that are left out. It is deeply humiliating. I look at Rhona and Yuk Lan and wonder what we have in common.

Rhona, Yuk Lan and I have to take it in turns practising with each other. One-two-three, one-two-three, learn the pas de bas; learn the St Bernard's waltz. One-two-three. The good-looking boys and the pretty girls look over their dancing shoulders at us with disdain. We are clumsy girls, I'm being the boy today, we are stamping around awkwardly whilst the gorgeous couples glide and turn with exquisite ease. It is deeply embarrassing. I hate the St Bernard's waltz. It's stupid. One-two-three. There are three more girls in our class than boys. Sometimes, when it's girls' choice, I get to run across the hall and pick my favourite boy. He never looks very pleased to be picked by me.

I decide to pretend to be sick next week, and to avoid going to the school dance. Everyone thinks they are something special and they are not. They just look stupid dancing those silly old-fashioned dances. Nobody knows how to jitterbug or jive or jump in between legs like my dad does with my pal Gillian who loves jazz and blues. At lunchtimes, Gillian and I hang out together, play old records on her gramophone, Pearl Bailey, Tired of the life I lead, tired of the blues I breed. We're different from everybody. The school dance pretends to be about our enjoyment, I say to Gillian smoking a Sobranie cigarette for added sophistication. It pretends, but actually it is a form of control. Aye, so it is, Gillian agrees, blowing a perfect smoke ring with her pink Sobranie. Then she leans towards me and we kiss. Her lips are perfect. They could be a drawing. She's very good at drawings. She's good at kissing too.

Hilton Hotel, Milton Keynes

The first time I met my mother it was also in a hotel. I sat in the waiting area near the reception and waited and waited. I told the receptionist that a woman would be calling for me, an Elizabeth Fraser, and told her where I'd be sitting. I didn't tell her that the woman I was waiting for was my mother and that I'd never met her before, though half of me longed to blurt that out to the receptionist, perhaps to make it seem more believable. I still wasn't sure my mother would definitely turn up, since we'd made several dates to meet over a three-year period, and she had kept getting cold feet. We were meant to meet in the winter of 1988, months after my son was born, then the spring of 1989, then the autumn of 1989, then the summer of 1990, and now it was the autumn of 1991. I had a three-year-old son by then. The first letter I ever received from my birth mother arrived three days before I gave birth to my son.

I'd become very curious about my birth mother when pregnant, perhaps prompted by all the medical questions that doctors ask you. Do you know which diseases are in your family? What diseases run down your line? I started to trace her then at the age of twenty-six and had managed to find her sisters in Nairn in the Highlands. They'd said they would forward a letter from me to her and that I should wait to hear, and I finally did hear just before Matthew was born.

It's a bit like a blind date, waiting to meet your birth mother. I didn't know exactly what she looked like, though I'd been sent out-of-date photographs. I kept getting up from the leather-sofa seating area, and hanging around behind the glass partition to the hotel entrance. My mother could be any woman coming through the revolving door of the hotel. She could be somebody I've already passed in the street, or sat next to on a train, or held the door open for in a shop. She could be somebody I'd just missed, who had got on her train at Euston an hour before I arrived, somebody *I'd just missed*. It's freaky and alarming to think that you could have met your mother already and not even known. Because the truth is your mother is a complete stranger. She could be anyone out there. Before you found her she could have died. You wouldn't have known. Nobody would have told you; nobody would have known where to find you because you are a complete stranger too. You are both relative strangers.

My heart is fluttering. I think I should know her. I think I should recognize her the minute she comes through the door. Will she choose the revolving door or the sliding door? There's much that's peculiarly romantic about the waiting. What will her hair be like? What will she be wearing? What will her walk be like? Will she bring me a present? Will she hold me close and cry? Will she be wary, cold and distant? The sensation I am most filled with though is not anticipation, but dread. I'm terrified. I feel as if it is all going to go horribly wrong. I'm terrified of meeting my mother. I'm not sure what calamity I think might happen, but if I hadn't arranged it all, I might run off. I suddenly understand all the cancelled dates. It takes some bravery to stay put. The clock ticks. She is now late: five minutes late, then ten minutes. All the waiting minutes are equally slow. Perhaps she's not coming. If she doesn't come, that might be a relief. I think to myself that if my mother *does* turn up, it will mean that she too has used all her courage to come and meet me.

Finally, a woman comes through the sliding door that I think might be her, except that she's with another woman much younger than her. The woman that I think might be my mother is carrying a plastic bag, a huge panda and a bunch of orchids, which is weird because I too am carrying a bunch of orchids. She's small in height, even smaller than me, and has reddish hair. She's quite well built, not as big as me, but not slight either. She's wearing a cream raincoat and a black-and-white scarf. 'Jackie?' she says and hugs me. Her eyes fill with tears. I expected tears might come to my eyes, but they don't. I would like to be able to cry. What is the matter with me? I hug her back and feel a little numb. 'This is Jenny from my church,' she says, introducing me to a thin young woman with straggly hair.

'Hello, Jenny.' I shake her hand.

'I'm just leaving. I'll be back for her in an hour,' Jenny says to me, as if my mother was a child and I was a worker in a crèche. I almost go to joke, 'I'll have her ready and her nappy fresh,' but I don't. Jenny gives Elizabeth a huge sideways smile of encouragement, and then takes her leave back through the revolving door, waving until she's disappeared.

Elizabeth and I go and sit down in the hotel's reception area on the big grey leather sofas that are facing each other. It doesn't feel right, but my hotel bedroom has Matthew and Louise my flatmate in it and we only have an hour, so there's no point trying to find somewhere less soulless. I've waited for years to meet her so I don't want to squander a single second. We sit down on the big grey sofa and Elizabeth hugs me again. She takes my hand and pats it. Her eyes are still full of tears. She says, 'I brought this for Matthew,' pointing to the panda, and we exchange bunches of orchids, laughing at the coincidence of the flowers. A little unnerving: I wonder if that choice has anything to do with genetics.

'I'll go and get him down in a bit so that you can see him,' I say. She opens the buttons on her raincoat and takes it off, folding it on the seat beside her. She's wearing a black-and-white cardigan and a smart black skirt. Her knees look round and vulnerable.

Elizabeth folds and unfolds the empty carrier bag in her hand, troubled, and anxious. 'Jenny came with me for moral support,' she says, and I nod. It doesn't seem appropriate to bombard her with questions about myself, and everything that I was burning to ask her has suddenly left me. I can't think what I'd like to know. Opposite me is a woman in her fifties, quite well turned out, wearing a nicely patterned scarf. I can't see anything of my face in hers. Her lips are quite thin. I find myself staring at her features in a way that is probably unseemly. She's brought photographs of her children with her, and she shows me them. 'This was Royce,' she says sadly. 'He was a handsome boy. This is Aisha. This is Chloe.' I scrutinize the photographs. Her children are all the same colour as me because she has married a dark-skinned man from Singapore. I'd always imagined they would be white, with red hair, but they are not. They all have black hair and brown skin. One of her daughters, I think, looks a bit like me. I show her the ones I've brought. I've tried to select the photographs so that I can show her my life in pictures. There's me and my brother and my dad on the Isle of Mull. I'm four and we're playing at being Scottish soldiers. There I am, in Jessie Clark's back garden, doing a show, whilst my brother digs at a tree behind him. Me in a white dress, aged three, with my head thrown back laughing. There's my mum and me, me wearing a brown anorak, identical to my brother's blue one, on the ferry to Mull. There's me in Abercromby Place, Stirling, a student with an Afro. There's a photograph of my mum and dad in their thirties. My mother stares at my parents for ages, and says they don't look like how she imagined them to look. She sounds faintly disappointed.

63

She asks me how my work has gone in Milton Keynes, and I remember that I've lied to her and told her I was there for some other purpose in order finally to get to meet her. 'Fine,' I lie, through my teeth that don't look like her teeth at all. 'It's not been too difficult.'

She nods. 'You're obviously a hard worker?'

'Quite,' I say, a little uncomfortable with my whopper.

Then my mother spends the rest of our hour telling me about her neighbour's heart problems: once she starts on this subject, she can't stop. I want to interrupt and ask her things, but I don't have the heart. After a while, I say, 'What was he like, my father?' and she says, 'I can't really remember. It was a long time ago.' She giggles, secretively, as if she *has* just remembered something, but can't tell me.

'He was musical,' she says, nonchalantly. 'I remember that. He was kind. I think he was in a band.'

I like the idea of this, and turn it over. 'What kind of band?'

'I'm not sure,' she says vaguely.

'What instrument did he play?'

'I can't remember.'

'But he was musical?'

'Yes, definitely musical.'

Well, that's nice. Then she returns to telling me about her neighbour's heart. I feel a little foolish really – what was I expecting? What kind of conversation can you sensibly have? It's almost as if the weight of it sits between us, a third person, or perhaps a small child with her mouth closed shut. The hour that I'd thought would be very short, starts to stretch and seem quite long, like the visiting hour in a hospital. We don't really know how to converse. There's an uncomfortable intimacy between us; the knowledge that we are biologically mother and daughter makes me feel a little like a fraud. We haven't earned the right to call ourselves anything really. I like the fact that Elizabeth has always called herself Elizabeth to me, and never tried anything else.

When I was a young girl, I used to imagine my birth mother was Shirley Bassey. Every time I watched her on telly singing 'Goldfinger', I'd point my finger and shout, 'That's her!' Then I found out that my birth mother was a white nurse from the Highlands and I was disappointed. That memory, Shirley singing 'Hey Big Spender' and me being convinced she was my mother flashes seductively before me. As long as he needs me . . . No regrets . . .

Every so often I see Elizabeth dart me a look. I try and read it. It's like learning Braille. Of course we don't know each other at all, though I've heard of people who meet their birth parents and feel an instant sense of recognition. 'Do you think we look alike?' I ask her.

'You've got something of the Frasers around the mouth, definitely,' she says. 'You look a bit like my youngest daughter.'

'Isn't it funny we both brought each other bunches of orchids?' I say and she nods and says, 'They're nice flowers, orchids, they last quite a while.' I want to carry mine home and look after them so that they live for days.

I might spray the leaves, and make sure they sit in an easterly window, and keep them out of the direct sun. They look tender, vulnerable almost, like her knees. The clock is ticking; the last ten minutes start to come in quite quickly; time changes its tempo. I have so many questions but it now seems worse than inappropriate, it seems ill-mannered for me to ask them, to drag Elizabeth back to a painful time in her past, a time she clearly doesn't want to remember, just to satisfy my own curiosity. 'How long did you keep me for as a baby?' 'Did you breast-feed me?' 'How long for?' Or worse, 'Did you have a lot of pressure put on you to give me up for adoption? Are you happy I traced and found you? Did you ever expect to hear from me?' They all seem cruel questions, selfish, indulgent, so I don't ask them. I know what having a baby is like now; and yet I cannot possibly imagine what it would be like to give my baby up. I go up to my hotel room and get Matthew, who is playing with Louise. 'Come and meet Elizabeth,' I say to Matthew. I bring him down and Elizabeth bobs her only grandchild uncomfortably on her lap and gives him the giant panda. She says, 'He's my grandson,' as if that thought has only just properly occurred to her. The panda is bigger than Matthew. He's delighted, amused by its size. He laughs holding it by one of the panda's black-and-white hands and tries to twirl it. Elizabeth's eyes fill again. 'He's a handsome boy, aren't you a handsome boy?' Perhaps Matthew reminds her of her own son as a boy. Elizabeth is impressed when Matthew says, 'Tank you.' But I think he's thanking her for the panda.

A few minutes later, Elizabeth's church friend Jenny is back to collect her. I walk through the hotel's sliding door and wave her goodbye. She's carrying her orchids and some photographs of me as a child that I've had copied for her. She looks relieved, as if whatever it was she feared was going to happen didn't, as if she didn't really need her church escort. Perhaps she imagined I might have got out of control, or been angry, or shouted in her face. It's hard to tell. She doesn't know me, after all, any more than I know her. I could have been a raving lunatic. I could have been bitter and accusatory. I could have sat sobbing on the hotel sofa for an entire hour.

In the weeks after that first meeting, I felt jangled and upset by it. I cried on and off for the best part of three weeks, unable to understand the extent of my distress. I couldn't understand what exactly was so upsetting. It was like a kind of grief; only I'm not sure that I was grieving my birth mother, I think I was grieving the imaginary mother I'd had in my head. The one who was madly in love with my father, a handsome cross between Paul Robeson and Nelson Mandela, the one who danced and danced in the Aberdeen ballroom in a black-and-white polka dress, who tossed her thick hair and wore bright red lipstick, who had been broken-hearted when my father had had to return to Nigeria because he was *betrothed*. The story I had put together in the intervening years was not the woman who came through the sliding door in the Hilton Hotel in Milton Keynes. My birth mother was a sad and troubled figure; she'd had a hard life, been in and out of psychiatric hospital, had numerous breakdowns, and survived a son's suicide. I felt a terrible sadness for her life; that somehow, at her expense, perhaps, I'd got lucky.

There was nothing euphoric about our first meeting. It felt muted and mellow; there was too much to say and too little that was said. Maybe it's possible to grieve for the relationship you never had? It's hard to know what the terrible sadness was caused by exactly, and it took me by surprise. It wasn't as if I regretted being adopted: I didn't; it wasn't as if I'd had an unhappy childhood: I hadn't. I felt so alarmed and frustrated with myself. Elizabeth's life, the sadness of it, was overwhelming. Just as she'd wished the right parents for me, and prayed for my happiness, I had wished that she'd had a happy life, kind daughters and intuitive sons.

The next time I met Elizabeth was about four years later in the autumn. This time I didn't pretend I was coming to Milton Keynes for any purpose other than to see her. I asked her to pick the place because the formality of the hotel had made her uncomfortable. She picked the cafe in Boots the Chemist inside the Milton Keynes main shopping centre. When I got there she was sitting on a bench outside Boots but inside the mall. We both went up the escalator, together, to the Boots cafe. I hadn't been on an escalator with my mother before. It felt quite novel. I was behind her looking up as the stairs carried us to the cafe; it gave me a couple of minutes to adjust to meeting up again. At the Boots cafe counter, we both ordered soup and a roll and butter and herb tea. The woman behind the counter said to Elizabeth, 'Your table is still there,' and pointed over towards the window, smiling in an overly kindly way. Elizabeth looked a little embarrassed. I realized that she'd been up earlier to make sure that we got to sit at her favourite table that looked out the window and down to the fancy internal water fountain inside the shopping centre. I found that touching, that she wanted a table with a view of an artificial fountain. When we got settled, she said to me, 'I like the view here.' I was nervous this time too, and I could see that Elizabeth was also, though I felt much more comfortable than the last time. Elizabeth actually looked excited to see me, and looked as if she liked the sight of me. She'd brought more photographs this time of her dead son, and her two daughters, and her sisters in the Highlands. She was disappointed I hadn't brought any. I was annoyed at my own lack of thought. I hadn't realized that it was something she would like to do every time we met, swap photographs of the intervening years, a photographic catch-up on a life.

She told me that she drank herbal tea because the Mormons didn't believe in caffeine, which I hadn't known, and that she didn't drink alcohol or smoke cigarettes, also because of her religion. I told her that I smoke and drink and she looked troubled for me, which was gratifying. She told me that the Mormons believe that adopted people ask to be adopted whilst still in the womb and that she believed the perfect parents had been found for me because she'd prayed for them. I tried to picture the embryonic me, knocking on the wall of her uterus, shouting, *Oi, you, can you get me adopted?* It was so preposterous it almost made me laugh. But she had said it quite seriously; and on the other hand, I had always felt *fated* to be with my mum and dad. What was the difference between my sense of fate and her Mormon God? Elizabeth obviously needed to believe in the Mormon theory of adoption; it assuaged the need for any guilt and shifted the burden of responsibility to me. But I don't think Elizabeth was telling me her theory in order to blame anybody; she was saying it because for her it wasn't so much a belief by now as a simple statement of fact.

I told her they were the perfect parents, and she nodded again pleased. 'I knew they'd be right for you,' she said with total, almost enviable, conviction, 'I just knew it.' But I remembered her studying the photograph of my parents on our first meeting. 'They don't look how I imagined.' She had sounded slightly disappointed. 'What did you imagine?' I remembered saying a touch defensively. 'I'm not sure,' she had said, her voice wavering, '. . . *taller,* maybe? I was told that your father was in the army and that you would be being brought up abroad.' I laughed. The idea of my dad in the army was quite hilarious to me. I wondered if the adoption people deliberately made this up so that she wouldn't ever try and find me. In 1964 she was living in Glasgow. Had she known I was living there also she might have been uncomfortable. Perhaps those rules were to save people driving themselves crazy.

Something about the way she hesitated before saying

taller indicated that that *taller* wasn't the word she was actually thinking. Perhaps she wanted to say richer, more groomed. Perhaps she imagined my dad to be a tall army officer and my mother to look chic and slim and beautiful. Though my parents are a handsome couple, to Elizabeth perhaps they looked too ordinary. Everyone involved in adoption has an imaginary version of everyone else. My mum also imagined my birth mother to be tall and beautiful and was expecting me to be tall too. She'd say when I was growing up, 'Your feet are big and your hands, I think you're going to be tall, Jackie.' She imagined my birth mother had been a young girl when she'd had me, no more than twenty certainly and probably about seventeen. She imagined my father to be tall too, tall and handsome and dark, maybe a bit like Sidney Poitier, she used to like saying, 'I picture a Sidney Poitier figure.' My birth mother had obviously imagined my parents to be from a middle-class background and thought that they would be very attractive too. Whoever imagines the ugly? I wondered. Who imagines the wee people?

When I first spoke to Elizabeth on the phone, she laughed and said, 'Oh, I didn't expect you to have a Glasgow accent.' Her Highland accent had gone completely. She had a high voice, very light and girlish-sounding, as light as froth, and an English accent, which surprised and disappointed me. I thought she'd have a lilting Highland accent, might even know a bit of Gaelic. I thought *she'd* have hung on to her tongue. But then she felt Scotland had let her down. 'Scotland is very racist,' she said, sipping at her soup in Boots that day. 'Did you have any problems at school?' she asked me.

'Sometimes, but my mum and dad always went straight to the school and complained. They were my champions.'

'I often had to go and complain as well for Royce and Aisha. I hate prejudice, don't you?'

'Yes,' I said.

'And you were happy?' she said, tentatively, afraid of my sadness more than her own.

'Yes, very happy.'

Elizabeth nodded, absolved by me, for a moment, it seemed.

'I was a very happy wee girl. I still am a happy person,' I said.

'I can see that,' she said and took another serious spoonful of soup. I asked her if her daughters had problems with their weight, and she said, 'Chloe is quite big, though not as heavy as you,' but she said this in a kindly way. It didn't make me feel judged, though it did make me feel morbidly obese. We hugged and left each other for another five years.

The next time I met Elizabeth, I had arranged in advance to take her out to lunch. It was near Christmas time 2001. I first of all arranged to meet her outside the library in Milton Keynes, and then I changed my mind and decided to treat her to lunch in a nice Italian restaurant I'd found. I sent a letter telling her of the change of venue in plenty time. I got to the restaurant on time but Elizabeth wasn't there. I cursed myself for changing the meeting place. I thought maybe she'd gone to the library so I phoned the library and asked them to look on their steps and see if a woman was waiting and ask her if her name was Elizabeth. A kind librarian did this and then phoned me back. 'No,' she said, 'no one is there.' 'Should we send a message on the loudspeaker in case she is actually in the library?' the librarian asked me.

'Yes, please,' I said.

She came back in a bit. 'No luck, I'm afraid.' Then she said, 'Excuse me, but I recognize your voice from the radio. You're not Jackie Kay?'

'Yes,' I said, thinking, I don't bloody believe this.

'Your *Adoption Papers* is one of my favourite books,' the librarian said.

'Thank you,' I said. 'Thanks very much.' The irony was not lost on me. It was my mother who was lost.

I phoned Carol Ann, in some distress, saying, 'I can't find Elizabeth. I don't know where she's gone. She's not come to the restaurant and she's not in the library. They even sent a message for her on their loud-hailer.' Carol Ann rang the number we had for her, and somehow managed to get through, though I had been ringing it and had not got through, and told Elizabeth where to meet me. Elizabeth arrived in a very bad temper, as if I'd tricked her. When I asked her where she'd been waiting for me, she said that she'd just gone and stood in the middle of Milton Keynes Shopping Centre, though she *had* actually received my letter telling her of the Italian restaurant. I didn't understand this, and Elizabeth being in a temper perplexed me. It was as if she thought I'd done something deliberately wrong. The confusion about the meeting place spoiled the lunch, and I was left thinking, Why bother with this? She might be my birth mother but that doesn't mean I have to like her. I decided I probably wouldn't see her again. It was all too confusing and upsetting.

That time, because it was near Christmas, she bought me two empty bevelled glass frames as a present. I brought photographs to show her, mainly of Matthew, getting older. 'He's a big boy now,' she said. 'I remember knitting him that little yellow jacket, for when he was first born, did you like it?' I nodded. 'I knitted something for you,' she said, 'did you know that, and then I sent it to the Adoption Agency who promised they would send it on to your mother. It was a lovely little outfit, a pink and white cardigan, and little boots.'

Next time, eight years later, Elizabeth asked to see *me*, and seemed anxious to set up a meeting quickly. This time, she wanted me to come to her house. The suggestion of her house for the first time ever felt an honour and a relief; we were not going to greet each other in another public place, hotel reception, Boots the Chemist or Italian restaurant. It meant that we might have progressed somehow; we were no longer interlopers running into each other in peculiar places like cold-war spies, exchanging strange parcels. It meant that she trusted that I would not just turn up at her door at odd hours: the doorstep is a significant place for the birth mother, and every birth mother must either dread or pray for the long lost appearing on it. I was interested to see what kind of house she lived in.

I knew before I got there that Elizabeth was having problems with her memory because she'd sent me five birthday cards, each one forgetting the last. She'd also sent my son five Christmas cards, each one with a ten-pound Marks and Spencer Gift Voucher in it. He came up with a plan to return them and sent her a Christmas card with some of the vouchers back. Matthew had thought I'd been exaggerating when I told him of Elizabeth's memory loss until those cards had kept coming every couple of days from December 1st up until the few days before Christmas when he conceded, 'I see what you mean, Mum.' Somehow I sensed that the urgency about the meeting had to do with her memory, as if she had to see me again before she forgot she'd had me adopted, or before she forgot that I existed, or whilst she could still be herself enough to have a conversation.

I wondered if the memory confusion had already started the last time we met, and that that was the reason she'd just gone and stood in the middle of the shopping centre, and that too would explain the paranoia and anger. I wondered in the taxi on the way to her house in Milton Keynes whether or not she'd remember that I was coming.

We went round several small roundabouts with civic

displays of flowers and then turned right down one small street and left down the other. There, on the doorstep of a very small terraced house, the one on the corner of the street, stood Elizabeth. She had remembered. And she was standing with the door open before I even got out of the taxi. She was beaming, a lovely big open smile, and one that I'd never seen on her face before, as if her memory loss had allowed a softer version of herself. I felt a rush of shyness, and that same nervousness. I tried to look stylish getting out of the taxi, un-clumsy and unfettered. I gathered my bags, her flowers and her presents and gave her a hug at her front door. She hugged me back for ages, tears in her eyes, and this time, there were tears in mine. We went through to sit in her living room. The living room was curiously empty of anything except a kind of a shrine on the floor, a special cloth and some cards on it, many sent by me, and a low coffee table with framed photographs of her family. She showed me a picture of Matthew and me, unframed, but she said defiantly, 'I'm having you both out now. I've put you out on the table.' I felt quite pleased, after all the years of being shut up in the suitcase below her bed. The relief of the fresh air! Secrets are musty as mothballs.

'What will you say about us to your family?'

'I'll say you are friends,' she said. 'I wanted to put you out. I wanted your picture out.' And she nodded her head with great emphasis, as if there were other people who wanted our pictures hidden.

There was a tall wooden giraffe on the floor and apart

from that very little else that was personal. Elizabeth still, even in her own house, remained an enigma. I couldn't quite put her together, or relate her back to me. 'I listen to your poems,' she said. 'Your voice is comforting.' She took my hand and held it. 'I liked them. It's easier to listen to them than to read them.' Then she got up and led me by the hand to her kitchen, a small kitchen with no table in it to sit at. On the Formica shelf were a giant-size bar of Cadbury's whole nut chocolate, a box of Milk Trays, and a packet of chocolate biscuits, a packet of PG Tips, and a pint of milk. She pointed at them, and said, 'Look, these are the chocolates Ravi brought for you coming around.' She was pleased. Ravi is her ex-husband, who still obviously looks out for her and does not know that I'm her daughter, but knows that I'm her friend.

I nodded, and said, 'That was kind of Ravi.' We went back into the living room without her offering me either a cup of tea or a chocolate biscuit.

'I'm going to take you to my church for lunch,' she said. 'That will be all right, won't it? They do a good bowl of soup.'

'Yes, lovely,' I said. It was quarter to twelve. All over the living room little pink Post-It notes, reminding her of things, were stuck to every conceivable surface. *Check cooker. Milk. Phone Aisha. Church Homework. Jackie. Lock door. Check door. Turn off tap.* Then she showed me her Bible and told me that she hadn't done her homework yet, giggling a little like a naughty child.

'What sort of thing do you have to do for your homework?'

'Memorize scriptures,' she said, vaguely, 'but my memory's going. I get so frustrated and my daughters get angry with me. They all get angry with me for forgetting things.'

'It's not your fault,' I said. 'You can't help it.'

'Well, they think I can. What was I going to say again? Do you believe in life after death? I think my son is around. I can feel him.' She picked up a picture of her handsome boy and showed him to me. 'I feel close to him now; feel like he's at peace. He got involved with the wrong people, who were all only interested in money, money, money.' She stroked the picture of Royce as if he might, wherever he is, be comforted, as if he might already have changed back into a smaller boy who is being sung to sleep. Then she got up abruptly and took me to the kitchen again and showed me the chocolates Ravi brought for me coming. 'Did I show you the chocolates Ravi brought?' she asked me.

'You did, yes, that was kind of him,' I said, feeling my tummy rumble. We went back into the living room again. I asked her why she only had a mobile now and not a land line.

'Because they were listening in,' she said.

'Who?' I asked, feeling alarmed, and a bit scared.

'Them,' she said, darkly. 'They were listening in and sending me messages. I didn't like them.' At that point her phone rang; it was her daughter. Elizabeth got all agitated, wildly so, as if her daughter was a member of the Mafia. 'Aisha?' she said, her voice very high-pitched with anxiety, half shouting, holding the phone too tight to her ear, 'Aisha? I can't talk; I've got my friend here.' Her phone suddenly went dead. 'Aisha? Aisha? Nobody there. She's angry with me,' she said.

'Why?' I said, feeling a strange fury for this unknown, unmet sister that was making Elizabeth feel so frightened.

'I don't know, she's always angry. Angry I've got some-one here and can't talk to her.' The phone rang again. Again it was Aisha. Elizabeth got all agitated again, and I couldn't understand what was going on. Then she hung up. 'Perhaps she wants to speak to me?' I said to Eliza-beth. 'Maybe she doesn't believe you've got a friend here?'

'I often think about telling her about you,' Elizabeth said. 'But I think she'd be angry, very angry, and she'd tell her father. Those two are very close. Chloe would be nice, she'd understand, maybe. But Aisha . . . but I really should tell them.'

'I think it might be a lot better than you think,' I said, trying to sound casual about it all. 'Most people are pleased once they get over the initial shock, and they might like to meet me. They might even like me?'

Elizabeth nodded, away half in her own world by now, and said, 'Yes, I might tell them.' But then again she has been saying she might tell them for twenty years, so I don't hold out much hope. I imagine that when Elizabeth dies, these two sisters of mine will find twenty years' worth of letters and photographs of Matthew growing up and me changing into a middle-aged woman and wonder why I never got in touch with them directly. I imagine by the time my sisters find out about me we might be all in our sixties.

It's difficult for me to understand the extreme need for secrecy, except that in Elizabeth's case, and in Jonathan's, the secrets are bound up with God. Elizabeth tells me that she's asked God if she should tell her daughters about me, and God is starting to think that she should but has told her to wait for the right time. The mention of God reminds me of the promise of a bowl of soup. 'Shall we go out for our lunch, then?' I ask her.

'What time is it?' Elizabeth says, wildly disorientated. 'Quarter to one! Quarter to one! Why didn't you say something! Yes, you should have said!' She sounds a little angry with me. She gets up and rushes her coat over herself, and dashes around looking for her handbag. She finds it and digs in it till she uncovers her keys, triumphantly. We get out of the house and she very carefully double-locks her door, pulling it towards herself to check. Then she says, 'I must make sure I put my keys in my zipped pouch or I'll never find them.' I thread my arm through hers and we set off down her street. But suddenly she stops and says, 'I can't remember where my church is.' She looks completely confused. Perhaps somebody usually walks her to church or drives her. I'm no use to her because I don't know where it is either. 'I know,' she says, excitedly, as if she's devised a cunning plan, 'my hairdresser might know.' There's a hairdresser on the corner of the street next to her. Milton Keynes is like a toy town, like a made-up place, and the hairdresser is plumped in the middle of a residential area. Somehow it's unsettling, though I can't quite think why. Perhaps because the whole area has an air of unreality to it; people are playing at being alive, but not really alive. Perhaps because it is a new town, only forty-odd years old, a town associated with loneliness and soullessness; the settlement based on a grid designed to make living in it seem like filling in pieces of a crossword puzzle. A town with no history except that I'm in it now walking up and down the grid with the mother from my past. It is totally surreal. She opens the door of her hairdresser's, and turns to me and says confidently, 'They know me in here.'

'That's good,' but, I think, will they know her church?

'I can't find my church,' Elizabeth announces to the hairdressers. There are only two customers in there. One is under an old-fashioned drier that looks like a space helmet. And the other is having bits of tin foil stuck to her hair for highlights.

The young hairdresser with bright red nail varnish smiles and says, 'Which church?'

'I don't remember its name,' Elizabeth says.

And the young woman stares at her as if she is stark raving mad. 'Sorry,' she shrugs her shoulders. 'Can't help.'

We leave the hairdresser's and Elizabeth says to me, 'Aisha would be really angry with me by now. You're not, are you?'

'No,' I say and stroke her arm. 'I'm not angry. It's quite fun. We're going on a little pilgrimage to find your church.' Elizabeth chuckles.

A police car is stationary by the opening to a wooded area. She waves at the car and the policeman on the passenger side rolls down his window. 'I'm looking for my church,' Elizabeth says, with the urgency of someone who might want to report a missing child.

'Which church?' the policeman says.

'I'm not sure,' she says.

'Is it a big church? A big stone building?'

'Yes,' Elizabeth says, clutching at straws, 'yes.'

'Well, there's a big church over that way.' He gets out the car and points west. 'If you go along there, through the underpass, cross the road, you should find it.' So Elizabeth and I set off again, but in a few moments it's clear that she's not sure at all where she is again, and so she stops and asks another stranger, who seems quite confident about a church he knows and points us off in the direction of that one, to the east. Finally, it is nearly two o'clock and Elizabeth is really worried that by the time we find her church they will have stopped doing lunch and we won't get to taste the church soup. I'm ravenous, so I'm worried about not tasting the church soup too. We pass the corner of a building that Elizabeth recognizes, and then a tree that she recognizes too. 'That's it,' she points at the church in the distance, 'that's it,' but Elizabeth can't remember the right way in, and we walk around what turns out to be the wrong way round, and finally are at the canteen. It's an ordinary wee canteen, but, hallelujah, it is still open and still serving soup! Elizabeth and I order a bowl each and I order a baked potato with cheese and coleslaw because I'm fantastically hungry now. We settle ourselves with the soup, and Elizabeth sighs with relief and relishes her soup. She makes me feel that we are both at a feast or a banquet. 'Isn't the soup delicious here,' she says rapturously.

'It's very tasty,' I say, and it is. Elizabeth eats her soup carefully and delicately. She's not a messy eater. She smiles across the church canteen table at me as if at last she might be enjoying herself, as if finally, in her church, she feels at home.

'Does your mum like soup?' Elizabeth asks me.

'Yes, my mum and my dad both love a good bowl of soup. My dad is good at making his own,' I say, proudly. 'He likes putting in everything, red lentils, garlic, barley, and making endless varieties of Scotch broth.'

'Does he?' Elizabeth says marvelling as if a man making soup was something unusual.

Perhaps it is. Perhaps my dad is unusual in more than one way. I imagine what they'd all be like if they met – my two mothers and my two fathers. I don't think my mum and dad would like it really. It would all feel wrong to them. Though once, when I asked my mum if she might like to meet my birth mother, she paused and said, 'Yes, I would like to thank her, because face it, Jackie, her loss has been my gain. Think about it.' 'Yes, I am thinking about it,' I said to my mum, laughing.

When we've finished our bowl of soup, we have a cup of herb tea, peppermint tea for both of us. Then Elizabeth says, 'Ooooh, I must show you the shop,' and she proudly shows me the church shop, which sells an assortment of cards, candles, tea cloths, aprons, religious books and maps of the world. I buy two cards that don't have religious images or messages on them, kind of big Georgia O'Keefe flower-type cards. Elizabeth looks pleased that I'm buying cards from her church, which is my sly reason for buying them, I suppose; her approval, memory-ravaged as she is, is still important to me. 'You send a lot of nice cards,' Elizabeth says, 'I've got a whole suitcase full of cards from you.'

'I'll send you one of these when I get back home,' I say. Elizabeth laughs as if this is some kind of trick that the card itself can perform, turning up in two places at once, pulled from my sleeve on the day we found her church and turning up on her doorstep weeks later. I know though that by the time she gets the card I've sent her, she might have forgotten we were ever there in the card shop together.

When we get back to her house I give her a clipping from a newspaper that has a large photograph of me and Matthew on it. I'm wearing a fake pearl necklace and an MBE medal, and Matthew is wearing the Italian suit our friend Brendan gave him and a purple tie and shirt that I bought him for going to the Palace. The article is cut from a Scottish paper, and was sent down to me by my mum, who had been sitting in her hairdresser's when she opened it, and said out loud, 'Bloody Hell!' and her hair-dresser said, 'What is it?' and my mum said, 'It's my grandson and my daughter in the paper. My daughter's just got an MBE.'

'What a shock,' my mum said to me, 'to open the paper at the hairdresser's and have your physog staring out at me. It's a big picture, Jackie, half the page.' My mum was quite excited about it, even though she had refused to come to the Palace and wasn't keen on me accepting the MBE anyway. She said, 'I'm not going to the bloody palace to sook up to the Queen,' which had make me laugh. And my dad said, 'In my opinion, you should reject it, but it's your decision.' And I thought I must be the only person I know whose parents are so cool that they advised me to reject a medal from the Queen. I went with Matthew in the end, Matthew and my friends Nick and Maura.

I took the clipping and gave it to Elizabeth, who was equally impressed with the size of the picture. 'Can I hold on to it for now?' she said.

'Yes,' I said. 'If you remember to post it back, since I'd like to keep it for Matthew.'

She took me through to the kitchen, 'Did I show you the chocolates and biscuits Ravi brought for you coming?' she said.

'Yes, you did,' I said, 'Very kind of Ravi.'

She took me upstairs and showed me her bedrooms, which were stacked with clothes lying in plastic sheets on the bed, as if back from a funeral or the dry cleaners, and as if they'd never be worn again. 'I sleep in the smallest bedroom,' she said. 'It's more cosy. What was I going to say again? I forget. I forget. I forget.'

'Do you forget people?' I ask her.

'Not their faces, no, but their names. I wouldn't forget you,' she said as if sensing my unasked question. I was half thinking that people with Alzheimer's might have things they need to forget, things that they've always kept secret, whole children, whole middle-aged women. A pink Post-It note, stuck to her sideboard, said *Don't forget Jackie.*

Then it was time for me to go home and my taxi arrived to get me it seemed all too quickly. Out of the four times I've met Elizabeth, this meeting was the best. Somehow, her Alzheimer's made her more open, more truthful. There's a kind of odd poetry in dementia that picks out jagged, glittering pieces of truth, and makes you have to reassemble them. 'You have an open heart,' she'd said to me. 'You can sense things. I can sense things too.' It was the closest we'd ever been, and probably the closest we would ever be. It was as deeply satisfying as it gets – a hunt for a church, a bowl of soup.

I sent Elizabeth the card with flowers on it and reminded her to send back the newspaper clipping so that I could save it for Matthew. But I really regretted doing that, and wish I hadn't. I hadn't thought of the anxiety it might cause her.

A few weeks after that meeting, I got a letter out of the blue from Elizabeth's husband. He didn't mention me being her daughter, so I presumed she still hadn't told him, and therefore didn't know how to reply. In the letter he said that Elizabeth was worried about having lost something belonging to me. He said that she feared that somebody, some unknown person, came into the house in the dead of night and took her secrets. I read the letter several times to see if it was coded, if he actually was trying to tell me that he knew I'm her daughter. Part of her illness was to believe that people were out to steal her important things. In a way it is the birth mother's nightmare. Earlier in her life someone had come, made her sign secret papers and certificates and hand her baby over. Someone had already said the name you give this child won't be kept. Someone had already stolen her baby. How does somebody cope with the enormity of that secret in old age, except to develop a disease that allows you to forget?

The forgetting is maybe not what's important; it's more interesting what you still remember. How blazingly alive the past is. The colour of the wallpaper in the bedroom you had as a girl. It's not so much that you've lost your memory, more like you're submerged in it, like you're living in the brightly vivid underwater world of the past.

My birth mother's ex-husband's letter presented me with another dilemma. What to do? To write back and say, Tell Elizabeth not to worry, but by the way, I'm her daughter? I thought if he ever found out about me being her daughter he would think it odd that I'd been complicit. So I wrote to Elizabeth instead, and said, Don't worry about that newspaper clipping, I don't need it any more.

Since that time I constantly worry that Elizabeth might actually forget she had me adopted, or just forget. Sometimes, I would like her to forget. But then I'm assuming with forgetting there comes a kind of peace. What I've noticed from Elizabeth is that with Alzheimer's, forgetting gives no peace, no resolution. Forgetting is fraught with a terrible anxiety, the kind that is filled with unknowable and unsayable things, a blazing, burning of everything, and finally maybe a complete forgetting of the self.

Alzheimer's is terrifying. I've now become petrified that I might get it myself, or that I already have it. I'm scatty with my keys. I'm constantly losing or forgetting things. I'm constantly leaving the house and then having to return for the dog lead, when my plan is to take the dog for a walk. It's scary. Particularly so because I've read that early Alzheimer's is twenty per cent more easily inherited than late-onset Alzheimer's. And I've also read that you can get Alzheimer's in your forties. The one great and huge advantage to never tracing birth parents is that you can remain in blissful ignorance about family diseases.

I remember before I ever traced Jonathan or Elizabeth being in an optician's in Kilkenny in Ireland. The optician asked me in his broad Kilkenny accent, 'What diseases run down your line?'

I said, 'I don't know.'

And he said, 'And why is that?'

And I said, 'I'm adopted.'

'I see,' he said. Then he turned out the light and

peered into the back of my left iris and said in quite a dramatic Irish voice, 'Please God, thank God, you don't have glaucoma.'

Elizabeth's eyes on that last visit had an unfocused look, like somebody whose clock was set in the past so resolutely that the present appeared blurry. She stood on her doorstep and waved, and then looked uncertain as to what to do next. Then she appeared to remember that she had to go back into her house, and she did, and she shut the door.

I wished I could have given her some happiness, taken her away on a little holiday. I thought of the kind of daughter I am to my mum and dad, and I thought for the first time very clearly that my mum was right, it wasn't me who had lost a mother, it was my mother who had lost a daughter. I wondered if she would remember to feed herself, and who would look after her properly, and how long it would be before she would have to go into a home. All the way back to Manchester on the train from Milton Keynes, I wondered about how often Elizabeth lost her way to her church. A lost soul, she seemed to me, my mother. A woman who had first lost her baby and much later lost her mind. I stared out of the train window until the dark came down and covered the fields, and blacked out the cows and the sheep, and I still stared out of the dark window and all I could see every so often was little chinks of light coming from the cars on the road in the distance.

When I get home, I find a little pink heart-shaped

Post-It note, stuck inside the zipped part of my purse, which reads, *Jackie, Elizabeth loves you* which moves me to tears because I don't know if she's reminding herself or me, and because her little habit of hiding secret notes has surprised me with this sudden gift.

1987

The November night after Fred has driven me up the motorway from London to Hebden Bridge, to go to Lumbbank in Heptonstall, I dream that I'm pregnant. It was my birthday yesterday. I was twenty-six. I dream that I've given birth to a fox. In my dream, I'm out pushing my daughter the fox in a Silver Cross navy hooded pram. She's wearing a nappy, my daughter the fox, a terry-towelling nappy. She's beautiful. I'm proud and overjoyed to be her mother. Strangers stop me and look into the pram. When they see my daughter the fox, they say, Oh, she looks a lot like you. I smile at the strangers and say, Thank you. She does, doesn't she? She looks a lot like me.

On the way up north yesterday, we passed a dead fox on the motorway. It was just lying there, dead. I worried about what it meant. It wasn't like the fox in 'The Thought-Fox', no sudden hot sharp stink of fox, no neat prints in the snow.

Fred and I have talked about having a baby for ages. He saw me looking broody one day in a cafe in Lewisham when a beautiful little baby, who was being fed mashed-up banana, smiled at me from her high chair. He said, You look like you'd like to have a baby. I said, I would. And he said, I'd be happy to be the dad if you like. And ever since that time, two years ago, we've talked about this baby we'll have together.

Fred's hair has some red in it. He's a light-skinned black man with red hair and green eyes. I wonder if my baby will have reddish hair, or dark black hair, my brown eyes, or Fred's green ones. Fred says the mathematics is mind-blowing. It only takes one sperm out of one hundred and eight million to make a baby. I wonder which baby I'll have. I know that he or she will be one in a million to me.

Nicon Hilton Hotel, Abuja

'Now,' Jonathan says, staring at me dazed and spent and dripping with the divine sweat of the two-hour service. 'Now,' he says, mopping his soaking forehead with a handkerchief. 'Now the time is yours. Ask me anything. I will try and answer it.'

'First,' I say, 'I'll give you a gift.' I get his present out of the hotel safe – *don't even bother with the hotel safe.* I give him the gift. He looks as if he is trying to keep his natural excitement under wraps because, perhaps, the Almighty has told him not to be too interested in material things. He opens the wrapping paper, slowly, with some enjoyment, and then he peeps in the box.

'This is very generous of you. This is very kind,' he says looking at the silver watch. He tries it on. It is too big. His wrist is thinner than I'd calculated back in Arthur Kay's Jeweller's in Manchester. I'd asked the jeweller to remove three links, but I should have asked him to remove five or six. I'm sad it is not exactly right. Jonathan says, 'No, it fits perfectly!' I tell him he can take it to any jeweller and they will take out another couple of links, but I doubt somehow that he'll go to the bother of finding a jeweller when he gets back to Enugu. 'No, no. It fits fine. It is a very nice watch. How much did it cost?' I try and shrug this question off politely, but he pushes. 'How much, tell me. I'm curious to know what a watch like this would cost.' He is still staring at the solid silver bangle, loose on his arm.

'A hundred pounds,' I say, giving in.

'A hundred pounds!' he whistles. Then he says, 'Now I have a question for you. Would you mind very much if I gave this watch to my wife?'

I'm stunned. 'Yes, I would mind,' I say. 'I bought the watch for you. It is a gift for you. I like to think of you wearing it and that you might sometimes think of me when you look at the time.'

'I don't need to wear your watch to think about you,' he says.

'That's nice,' I say touched, 'but I'd still prefer you kept the watch.'

'It's only that I have a watch already and my wife doesn't have a watch,' he says.

'Well, why don't you give her the watch you have and keep the watch I've given you?'

'This is a good solution,' he says. 'I didn't think about that. This is what I'll do. But now you must make up a lie for me to explain the watch. How would I get it? How would I have come across such a watch?' I feel oddly flattered by this; in a way it is the most intimate conversation we have had yet. It involves a joint lie! He's told lies to come and meet me and now needs more lies to return

94

home with the unexplained Seiko watch ticking on his arm. Perhaps all lies are fixed to some timing device that will eventually explode.

'Who did you say you were going to meet in Abuja? Religious people? Students? Whoever it was, tell her that somebody who admires your work had been given this watch from a friend in England as a present. That somebody didn't need the watch and it didn't fit them so they wanted you to have it.'

He nods sagely and says, 'This is a good lie.' I shrug. I'm not sure if it is or not. The face of the beautiful watch looks nonchalant on his hairless arm.

'Now,' Jonathan says, 'I have a gift for you too.'

I feel thrilled. 'You do?'

'Yes,' Jonathan says and pulls from his plastic carrier bag four born-again Christian leaflets. 'Save the orange one for last,' he beams. That one is entitled *Now that you have received Christ.*

'Thank you,' I say as graciously as I can muster. I still have my four different-coloured leaflets, the tiny jackets of many colours, wee Jacobs. They are the only things my father ever gave me. You have to count your blessings; one, two, three, four. The first is bright lime green, with a picture of Mount Sinai on it; lush purple clouds unfurl behind the mountain. The mountain is on fire, presumably with the glory of God. The small leaflet is A5 in size and quite filthy. The title is: *Behold the Glory of God!* On the first page, I glance over a paragraph which says: 'I see a time when the intensity of God's glory will dominate our Fellowship meetings and conferences, just like His Presence dominated a youth meeting I witnessed at the Mayo Hotel in Tulsa, Oklahoma, at a Crystal Ballroom where 200 youth, men and women, took off their shoes in the presence of God. The Holy Spirit was so powerful in that ballroom that the youth fell on their faces before God . . . for two solid hours!'

The taking-off of shoes and the two-hour service is not all that unusual then. It must have been very disappointing for Jonathan after all that effort that I didn't fall on my face in front of God or even venture to take off my Birkenstocks. 'You will eventually be ready to receive God, and when you are, read this one,' Jonathan says, flapping the bright orange leaflet. 'I think I'll put them away somewhere safe,' I say and pick the leaflets up gingerly, and put them in the front flap of my suitcase.

Now that we have no service on which to focus our attention, we are awkward in my hotel bedroom. I sit down in the chair next to him and give him the letter Matthew's written for him. 'That's nice,' he says, scanning it without much interest. I ask him to tell me as much as he can remember about his days in Aberdeen in the sixties, about how he met my mother, about whether or not he fell in love with her, and about how he found Scotland then, what it was like, friendly, and if he had to return to Nigeria because he was betrothed. Although he has said I can ask him anything, he seems perplexed about the idea of himself in the past, as if he was so totally somebody else then, he can hardly understand or remember himself, or hardly even believe that that Jonathan actually existed. It seems the younger man belongs to the strange hazy haar of the pre-born-again days; this one exists now; and now is the moment of the Lord. *Now* has total clarity. The past is a pea-souper. He is bored by the distant, hazy memory of himself. He recites tiny facts, dutifully, to try and please me. He tells me that he went to Dundee University too and to Oxford, and that he went to Aberdeen as a post-graduate student. The only light that comes shining into his past is his love of music. He played the bongo drums in a band called Los Latinos; the bongos made him popular with the women. He drums lightly, smiling, on the table in my hotel room. His hands are quite beautiful. I find myself transfixed by his long fingers. He says he met Elizabeth when she came one time to hear him play, though she says they met in a ballroom in Aberdeen.

Jonathan can barely remember anything about Elizabeth, not even what she looked like. He tells me his studies were the most important thing and that he saw her for a couple of days after she returned from the Mother and Baby Home in Edinburgh when I was born. Elizabeth had told me that she'd spent two weeks with him in Aberdeen and that he'd been very kind to her after my birth. 'Two weeks? No, no, no. The university would have never allowed me to share my digs for so long. Two days. Two days more like.' He tells me he was called up by the social services and asked to provide a name for me, so he suggested Joy, the name on my original birth certificate. 'Call her Joy,' he remembers saying, and left it at that. I ask him if he had ever thought about me at all over the years. 'No,' he says. 'No, of course not, not once. Why would I? It was a long time ago. It was in the past.'

In those days, he says, he was a sinner and enjoyed having a lot of fun, a man who loved his beer, his women and his drums. I wish I'd known him then! When I ask him again to tell me what he remembers of Elizabeth, he falls silent. He can't really remember her. 'I think she was a good-looking girl who liked music and was quite small in height. But when you first got in touch on the telephone, I wasn't sure I was your father. A lot of the women back then in Scotland liked the black men; they liked the Africans. They were busy going out clubbing, enjoying themselves. So the baby could have been anybody's.'

'But Elizabeth was certain. It was only you she slept with,' I say.

'Oh yes, there's no doubt about it that you are my daughter, you have my genes. And none of my children are dullards, but what I'm saying is at that time everybody was busy enjoying themselves.'

Earlier, I'd had a greedy swig of the cold white wine in the makeshift blue room church, but now I wanted to drink again, out in the open air. The claustrophobia of the hotel room was getting too much for me. I led Jonathan down to the outside swimming-pool area to order some food and wine. Once out of the bedroom, I felt better. Part of me felt happy, euphoric even. I looked into Jonathan's eyes and he looked into mine and for some moments I felt electrified and high. Here I was in Nigeria for the very first time at the age of forty-two, meeting my father. Meeting a birth parent stirs up such a strange mix of emotions; I wanted to fling my arms round Jonathan and run away from him at top speed.

We sat down and ordered some food. I ordered a chickpea soup, smoked salmon and a salad. Jonathan ordered hot pepper fish soup, Uncle Ben's fried chicken and chips. I ordered a bottle of cold white wine. Jonathan was about to order a Malt, a non-alcoholic drink, but then he paused. 'How much percentage of alcohol in a bottle of wine?' he asked me. 'About four per cent, do you think?' he said to me, nodding, wanting me to confirm.

'Something like that,' I lied. I thought, frankly, he might be more fun drunk than sober. And that turned out to be true: with a drink down him, Jonathan was more himself, and less like a messenger sent from the Lord. His habit of quoting incessantly from the Bible eased a little. But before he got stuck into the wine, he seemed to need one last big prayer fest. He told me he was a healer as well as a preacher. I said, cynically, and under my breath, 'Heal me, Jonathan!' And to my astonishment, he suddenly bounced into action, rushing across to my side of the table, putting one hand on my head, shaking my head back and forth with his fingers spread out all over my hair. 'You are a bundle of joy. All the people love you. You bring love into this world. O God Almighty, heal this woman. Take her to your bosom and clear her of any pain. Be with her and . . .' I closed my eyes. Here we go again. I quite liked the bundle of joy bit since Joy was the name he'd originally given me and it felt a little personal. 'These signs will follow those who believe. In my name they will cast out demons; they will speak with new tongues; they will take up serpents; and if they drink anything deadly, it will not hurt them; they will lay hands on the sick and they will recover. Mark 16:17, 18.' His fingers were now covering my face. I peeped out through the opening of one of the bars of his fingers into the bar area. A few sophisticated Nigerians drinking cocktails looked on bemused. Some looked a little irritated. Jonathan was not whispering either. His voice gathered and carried around the swimming-pool bar area as if it were a Greek amphitheatre. He was praying for me now very loudly and enjoying the fabulous spectacle that he was creating. In some strange way, he was intensely charismatic; perhaps he imagined that, like Jesus Christ, he was immensely attractive to the people.

This was the most physical Jonathan had been with me yet; I found his hand crushing down on my head, and shaking it back and forth too tight, too strong. He was practically crushing my skull. I hoped to God he would heal me, though, that I'd suddenly have a clean, good life, with a pure, good heart. I hoped the weight of my broken heart would get lighter. I hoped for once in my life to experience something miraculous! When he stopped, nothing felt any different. I was simply more acutely aware of people staring at us. I felt flushed, embarrassed, and grateful that I didn't know a single soul in the swimming-pool bar at Nicon Hotel, Abuja.

Jonathan sits back down at the table, quite relaxed, happy, the ceremony is over. Here he is with his new-found daughter, who is not a dullard, who is about to buy him dinner. 'You are good company,' he says to me, which surprises me because I've had no sense of being any company at all. Most unusually, for me, I've hardly opened my mooth!

'Am I?' I say, flattered.

'Yes, of course. You are good company. You are bright. You are charming. All is well with the world.' He asks me a little about my work. Do I do kind things? I tell him I work with old people and children and do all sorts of projects with poetry . . . I'm finding myself in the peculiar and maddening position of actually wanting his approval. My father says I am already doing the Lord's work without knowing it. No conversation can last more than a few minutes without the Lord being credited or complimented for something or other. God can be wildly praised and flattered; the rest of us must try to be modest, but God is a big-head. I try and accept that this is his way of talking, his way of seeing, and to see behind what he is saying, to listen differently.

Suddenly, the waitress who took our food order appears back at our table without the food. 'Father,' she begins, politely, 'I saw you healing the sister here. I am barren, Father. I wonder if you can heal me, please.' She is a very beautiful-looking woman, perhaps in her late thirties; perhaps she has been trying to have a baby for years. Her hair is woven on her head, like an intricate basket. She is tall, slim. Her very black skin glows in the sun. Jonathan is overjoyed. He springs to his feet and stands very close to her. He places his hands over her womb and starts the chanting. He can't quite believe how wonderfully God is arranging things for him today! The people in the swimming-pool bar area, trying to enjoy a pleasant Sunday dinner, look on aghast.

Then again, people here are used to these impromptu services; Nigeria is home to more splintered and fanatical born-again Christian groups than anywhere else in the world. Jonathan pats the waitress's stomach softly at first, then more vigorously, drumming on her stomach with both hands, as if he were playing the bongos. He asks God, in his mercy, to provide for her, to take away her barrenness and make her fertile. He says to her, 'You are a bundle of joy. All your family love you. You bring love into the world.' The same words he said to me; except for All Your Family Love You. I can't quite believe it, my father is a charlatan! Jonathan finishes his chant, opens his eyes and takes the beautiful stranger's hand in his. 'You will be pregnant by Christmas,' he says to her quite pragmatically, his voice dull and flat now, exhausted by the massive effort of it all. 'It will be a boy. Call him Jacob.'

'Thank you, Father,' the lovely woman says, tears in her eyes. She seems to really believe. 'Excuse me,' she says to me. 'I will go and bring your food now.' I wonder if the belief itself will be enough to end the barrenness.

Jonathan beams at me with real pride. 'God intended us to meet,' he says again. 'Everything is going well for me. I found a church in this hotel complex. I went to that service this morning. Then I gave you your service. And now I have healed you and I have healed this stranger. Do you see how she knew to come to me? She knew to come to me! People do this all the time, come up to me in the street. I heal many people. I use plants and roots, but it is God that does the healing.' He holds out his hands expansively, spoon in hand. Jonathan sits slurping his soup. 'So,' he says, 'you said in your letter that you didn't want to answer to a man. That is an odd thing to say.' He laughs his high laugh which is a bit like my laugh. 'So – if you are not married, and do not have a boyfriend or such, how do you cater for your sex drive?'

The question flies straight out of the blue African sky and flaps around me like a rare bird. I blink and knock back some more cold and indifferent white wine. I think to myself, What have I got to lose? I imagine that he'd think my lesbianism deviant, disturbed even, perhaps the sly work of Satan, but by this hour in the long day I have a devil-may-care attitude and couldn't care less if he gets up from the table and walks away or if he gets down on his knees again and asks me to repent. What the Hell, I think to myself, slightly inebriated, *bring it on*! Still, I hesitate a little longer, vacillating between bravery and cowardice.

'You can tell me. I am your father,' he urges, winningly. It is the first time he has said this simple sentence. He sees it working and repeats it with extra condiments. 'I am your father; you can tell me anything. I love you and I accept you because I am your father. There can be nothing that would shock me.'

It is the first time too that he has appeared really interested in anything about me. Just my luck. Not in my son, not in my childhood, not in my university days, not in my books, not in my parents, but in my *sex drive*! Fucking brilliant. 'Well, you know the woman you spoke to on the telephone?'

'Yes, yes, yes.'

'Well . . . she's my partner.'

'What do you mean?'

'She's my partner.'

'How so?'

'She's my lover. We've been together for fifteen years.' (I don't bother telling him that just before I flew to Nigeria, Carol Ann told me she didn't love me any more and wanted our relationship to end. Too complicated!)

'Oh-oh, oh-oh, oh-oh, oh-oh you mean you are lesbian?' He credits the word lesbian with three syllables with the emphasis on the last. *Les be an.* 'You mean you are *les be AN*?'

'Yes, that's right. I'm a lesbian.' Despite myself, I'm agog to see how he will take this news.

'OK-OK-OK-OK, OK-OK-OK-OK,' he says a string of OKs like prayer beads. Then very quickly he says, 'OK, OK. Which one of you is the man?'

'Sorry?' I say.

'I've often wondered about this,' he says. 'And I have never understood. How does it work? Which one of you is the man?' His eyes have acquired a sleazy shimmer. He is clearly having more fun than he's had all day. 'How is it possible for two women to have sex?' he asks me, asking me perhaps the most un-fatherly question I've ever heard.

'Neither of us is the man. It doesn't work like that.' I say, embarrassed. I down a whole half of a glass of wine. 'It's not like that.'

'So how do you have sex?' he asks. 'You can tell me now.' He leans forward.

I don't believe this: now the preacher wants a sermon on lesbian sex. It is too much. You never expect to talk to your father about sex, any father, adoptive or birth, about any sex, heterosexual or lesbian. But he won't let the matter drop. He keeps on. He reaches into the depths of his imagination for one final image. 'So what do you do? You squeeze each other's titties and so on and so forth?'

'And the rest,' I say under my breath, sweating now. I look at the turquoise blue of the pool with some longing. I would love to run along the diving board and take a beautiful, breath-taking dive into the pool. Not a belly flap. Not a lesbian belly flap – a beautiful fish arc of a dive.

Jonathan seems to sense that he is not going to get more salacious details out of me. Strangely enough, though, he has not been at all judgemental in the way I'd feared. So that's something. Quite the opposite. He says to me, 'When you get home, get out the Bible and say a prayer for each other in front of God, and God will recognize your relationship. I don't mind the women.

God doesn't mind the women. It is the men he minds,' Jonathan says, screwing up his forehead in disgust. 'It's the men who want to wear frocks that I mind.' I thought at first he was referring to transvestites, then I realized he meant gay bishops. There's been a split in the Church over the thorny issue of gay clergy, led by the fundamentalist Christians in Nigeria. 'The Bible says it is wrong, so how can they take up the frock?' Jonathan says, his face crinkling with revulsion. 'But the Bible says nothing about women.' His face smoothes out again. 'Anyway, it is better for you not to go with men. God intends you for higher purposes. It is better you are with women. Stay away from men. They will only give you Aids, and God wants you for himself. God has a unique plan for you.' Heavens, I think, now God is even involved in my sexuality! What a turn-up for the Book. 'Yes, God does not want you to waste time with men. God wants to keep you focused. Then your career will blossom.'

I go to my room to change my top. I'm sweltering hot in the purple silk top that I'd worn specially to meet him. I change into a brown-and-white sleeveless top, the brown and white stripes meet in the centre like an arrow. I go back down to join Jonathan at the bar. 'You've changed again!' he notices, and I realize it is the third time I've changed my clothes since we met a few hours ago. Perhaps I want to show off my entire wardrobe; perhaps I want to cover years. I suddenly remember the man on the aeroplane, from Manchester to Abuja, who told me that when I met my father he would give me an Igbo name.

I say to Jonathan, 'I've heard each Igbo child should have an Igbo name.'

'Ah yes,' Jonathan says, not nearly as interested in this custom as he is in lesbianism. He tries to feign some interest, to perform some outmoded African duty. 'OK, OK, OK, you could have one of two, which would you like? Either Ijeoma or Obioma. One means good journey and the other means good, kind heart. Which would you like to have?' he asks. 'You choose.'

'You choose,' I say. He has trouble choosing. So do I; it all seems a bit daft because he's not genuinely thought of it for himself; I've foolishly coerced him into it, perhaps out of a desire to be like Nigerian friends of mine, who have traced an original father and been given the late gift of a Nigerian name. Jonathan tells me I can have both if I want. Whichever I like. I pick the one that means good journey and check the pronunciation with him, repeating it whilst he wraps up some of the bread buns and some of his chicken to take back to his friend's house. '*Ijeoma*,' I say out loud, thinking about good journeys, from Manchester to Abuja, from Enugu to Aberdeen.

'This will do us for supper,' Jonathan says, happy at the sight of the food in his napkin. He sips some more wine. It is now nine o'clock in the evening. We have been together for seven whole hours. I tell him I have to be up the next morning to do my first workshop and reading for the British Council in Abuja. I call the soon to be pregnant waitress over and ask for the bill. 'I should be treating you,' Jonathan says. Then he says, 'Please do not make this into a negative thing. I don't want you to meet my children or to tell them about you. I have to keep you secret for my own reasons. But I have come here from my village and I have travelled on a bus for eight hours. I stayed overnight with an old friend. I could have denied you. I could have lied and not come to see you. I have acknowledged you between us and God. That is the most important thing. Nothing else matters. I can see you are my daughter. You have a kind face. I could tell from your photograph that you would be a kind woman. Make this a good thing. A happy thing.' I don't know how he knows to say that to me. I promise myself to try, to try and make it a happy thing.

We get up from the table and I walk him back to the reception, along the long corridor where we first met, it seems like ages ago now. We stop at the sad little bakery and I buy him two cakes to take back to his friend's house and two meat pies. He's pleased with this, appreciative. 'You are too generous,' he says. 'You are a dear and generous girl.'

I go to the desk at the reception and ask where Jonathan can get a taxi. I know I probably won't see him ever again. I'm not sure I really want to anyway. Once is enough, I think. You can't have two lives, just one. I shake his hand and try to hug him a little, but he's uncomfortable with that. He can only hold you properly when God is holding him. He shakes my hand firmly and says, 'Remain blessed. God will have his eye on you. You are protected now.' I think of rare birds, rare trees, of sanctuary. I think of secrets and lies and lives. I don't feel bitter or angry. I feel spent, exhausted. The skin on my face is tight like a mask. My head is buzzing. I stand waving at him as his taxi drives him away, until the black car carrying my father has disappeared altogether and I realize that I'm still standing waving at nothing. I go up to the blue bedroom and lie down on the needle-cord bedspread, the scene of the service years ago it seems. I picture a rare bird folding its wings. I picture Jonathan's journey back to his unnamed village, his new watch ticking on his old arm. I picture him travelling for eight hours on a bus to take him home.

1988

I have just felt my baby move for the first time. My baby turned and flipped inside me like a little fish. I am just beginning to show. My cheeks have more colour than usual. I don't feel alone. I feel my baby is keeping me constant company. There is not just one of me any more. There are two of us. I wonder if I am carrying a son or a daughter and what he or she will look like. I can't think of names that I like. If it's a girl, will I call her Helena or Genevieve? If it's a boy, will I call him Matthew or Lewis or Dominic? I wonder what it was like for my mother when she was pregnant with me. I wonder what she looks like.

I wonder what her name is and what her voice sounds like. I wonder what height she is, what kind of person she is. Is she still alive? It's the first time I've ever really thought real questions about her.

I decide I'll try and find her. The doctors keep asking questions about what diseases run in my family and I have to say, I don't know. I'm adopted. I decide that I'll try and get my original birth certificate, and trace her through that. It is a start. I want to know about the woman that carried me. I feel my little baby flip again. It is miraculous. Every time I see a pregnant woman in the street, she feels like a kindred spirit. I don't remember noticing so many pregnant women ever before. I can't get over it, the simple shock of it. Every single person I see on the street on any given day has been born. It comes to me as a revelation; something that I'd always taken for granted. Every one of us has been carried by somebody whether we know her or whether we don't.

23 July 2003

Dearest Jackie,

I was very happy to hear your news! You are more like my side of the family in looks. I have not felt well and am suffering from Angina for the past few months. Usually I rush around but I've had to slow down now. I'm not well at this present time!

I haven't got any doubts whatsoever. Jonathan is your birth father. I hope everything goes well for you in Nigeria. You can mention to Jonathan that I'm a Christian as well. I'm happy he has faith in God. I remember he used to mention, 'pray for you.' I did not have faith in those days, but I did pray and that is when I was told about your Mum. I realise now he must have had a religious background, so he is a very special person. I remember that he travelled to NAIRN with me on one occasion. Show him photographs of yourself as a little girl growing up. Tell Jonathan I'm sending my kind regards to him. Nigeria can be a very dangerous country so keep yourself very safe whilst your there. I'm happy to hear Matthew is doing well at school. My friend's son is 6ft 2 ins. She mentioned that when Matthew reaches 6ft he will stop growing.

I'm very tired now and I have stressful situations within this family! Aisha has now separated from her husband and lives in MK with Amy. I have been giving her and Amy moral support. Chloe works for the Emirates Air Line and is based in Dubai. She has travelled to many different countries. She liked Australia and mentioned that South Africa is a beautiful country. I have found it Very difficult thinking back all these years ago! Good luck with your stay in Nigeria.

Much love to yourself and Matthew.

From Elizabeth xx xx

PS I'm enclosing a photograph of myself taken shortly after my relationship with Jonathan.

PS I went to meet Chloe in Manchester about 6 months ago. We stayed overnight in the Hilton Hotel. I thought about you a lot but could not make contact. I don't like Manchester. It's a bit like London. Lots of Love Elizabeth xx

Mull

Remember the first time we went to Mull? You were four. Maxie was six and a half. You both had identical anoraks, yours was brown and Maxie's was blue. I sang to you on the ferry from Oban to Tobermory, *The Isle of Mull is of isles the fairest / Of Ocean gems 'tis the first and rarest / green grassy islands of sparkling fountains / of waving woods and high towering mountains*. Remember your brother boldly feeding the seagulls with the rest of his chips. He held his arm in the air with the chip between his fingers and they swooped down; oh they could be vicious. When we arrived in Tobermory, pretty harbour Tobermory, the local people gathered around you and your brother; they had obviously never seen anyone that looked like you, there was no harm in it, and they came up to me and said, Do they have the English? And I thought, Bloody cheek, most of you don't have the English, because a lot of them still only spoke Gaelic then. Remember how you loved that Mull Cheddar and ate blocks of it as if it were tablet or fudge? And that wee croft that we stayed in with the corrugated-iron roof and the outside cludgie? When we first arrived, I thought,

Oh dear, this is more than basic, how are we going to manage? Bare hard beds, bare floors. Pillows hard as concrete. But then we went and had one of the best holidays of our lives, so it just goes to show. Remember that eccentric Mrs Dungeon Bray who kept a shotgun and fired at any stranger on her land? She was a fierce old woman! Good job she was a bad shot! And the goat's milk that your brother and you both drank until you learned it was goat's milk and then suddenly didn't like it! We should have never told you! Oh, we had a great holiday there. There was Sam the Shepherd, a lovely gentle man, always dressed in big woolly jumpers, like his sheep. You used to do shows for me and your brother. You'd never bloody stop. You'd keep going for hours! Maxie would climb up onto the corrugated-iron roof and pretend he was in the gods, and I would sit below on the door step, and you, you would make up songs and sing them in that God-awful off-key voice of yours, and dance and dance, prancing up and down in your navy gym pants. Remember that ceilidh you and Maxie came to in the Balgie Barron and Maxie danced with that woman with the dark hair and Angus MacLeod had you up on the stage on his knee when he was singing and you were that embarrassed?

Remember the beautiful white sands of Calgary Bay? A strange thing about you: you never liked the feel of the sand in your feet. You would scream blue murder if you got sand between your toes, it was weird, weird, weird. We had to carry you over the sand. Maxie would disappear for hours fishing, and you spent hours with your face in a book or doing shows . . .

I'm at my parents' house, the house I grew up in, the house they have lived in for the past fifty-odd years. They are the only ones to have ever lived in it. When they bought it, it was brand new, a brand-new Lawrence house in suburban Bishopbriggs. They used to call Bishopbriggs *Spam Valley*, because they said the people living there were so aspiring to be middle-class that they couldn't afford anything but the house, so they had to eat Spam all the time. This was to distinguish it from a truly posh area like Bearsden or Newton Mearns. I'm sitting at the dining-room table that is placed in the extension. The extension was built when I was seventeen and had already left home. It still feels like, well, like an extension, like part of a new house tagged on to the old one, like limbo land. Now when I go home, my parents and I like nothing better than sitting round the table going over past holidays. Or they tell me over and over about their days in New Zealand, about the Cashmere Hills and the Bridle Path and the Routeburn track; about the Hamiltons, the idiosyncratic and talented engineering family my dad worked for: They invented the water-jet engine, tested the boat at the bottom of the Grand Canyon in Colorado to see if it could turn round on its own. Aye, interesting family; he always drove around in open-top Bentleys; in the winter he'd wear a balaclava. One of the family, Dick Georgeson, was the world gliding champion. Wasn't the wife an artist who had her own studio? my mum chips in. Or about the selfish girl my mum used to flat-share with, who borrowed all her clothes, and never paid a penny for anything, mean, mean, mean. I love hearing these stories, partly because they are familiar to me, and partly because I love the way they tell them in tandem, and both remember slightly different things. I envy the rare thing that my parents have, that they have shared over fifty years together and can keep each other's memories; tend to them, like a lovely garden with freshly blooming broom.

Every family holiday we went on, my dad would drive either the green Morris van or the white-and-grey Triumph Herald, or the blue Volkswagen Beetle. We always got beaten-down second-hand cars that lasted a couple of years. Whether we drove down to Devon or Campbeltown or up to Lochinver or Torridon, my dad would keep us entertained. Maxie or I would shout out a word and Dad would sing a song with that word in it. No matter how complicated the word, he always found a song. Once I shouted 'motor car' thinking he'd never find one, but he burst into singing 'Johnston's Motor Car'. The soundtrack to our holidays was my dad singing; and my mum joining in. We have sung our way all over Scotland. I remember shouting out 'road' on the way to Avielochan driving my favourite of the second-hand cars, the lovely Austin Cambridge, the beautiful light-grey car with red-leather seats, and my dad sang 'The Road to Dundee', 'Cauld winter was howling, o'er moor and o'er mountain / And wild was the surge of the dark rolling sea / When I met about daybreak a bonnie young lassie / Wha asked me the *road* and the miles to Dundee.' And sometimes he'd think of more than one song with the word in it, so would go straight into, 'It's a quarter to three, there's no one in the place except you and me, so give me just one for my baby and one more for the *Road*.' And when we shouted, 'Encyclopaedia!' he sang 'O Lydia, O Lydia The Encyclopaedia . . . the Queen of Tattoo', an old Marx brothers song. And when we shouted, 'Oil can!' he sang, 'Oh the sun shines bright on my *oil Can*tucky home,' to fits of laughter.

Now we sit around the table and play the holidays back: family holidays go quicker into the past than anything else; but also, peculiarly, stay in the land of a permanent present, quickly accessed with their fund of memorabilia and materials. Remember that caravan in Avielochan where the hens were so confident they came right into the kitchen and pecked at scraps of bacon, and I got my first period? So you did! You came running up to me and asked if you could tell your brother the special news. What age were you, eleven? Who was the friend you had with you again?

It was Claire Tomlins and she hadn't got her periods yet. I remember when I told her I was going to tell my brother, she said, better ask your mum if that's OK, as if there was something wrong with it, like it had to be some big secret. Did she? I remember we stopped off at the chemist's in Aviemore to get sanitary towels, which mum told me were like nappies. They are like nappies! I was disappointed in how meagre they were, how flimsy. I think I was looking forward to returning to being a baby. Don't talk daft.

And we sang our way to Torridon, driving in the green Morris Minor van. We stayed in a youth hostel in Torridon. Do you remember that Alsatian dog that belonged to the caretakers; it bit my hand really hard. I don't remember that! Yes, she's right, John, I remember. I got you some painkillers. And those owners weren't very nice about it, said I should teach my child not to stroke strange dogs? I don't remember that at all. Well, it happened if you both say so, but I would dispute it. I had the bite marks on my hand for years, just here remember, Mum, you made me lie down after I took the painkillers. I was thinking you might need an injection.

And we sang our way to Inverness, where we stayed with old comrades Mabs and Tummock Skinner who also had a mad dog, this time a collie, called Rufus, bright and intelligent, the source of my only Gaelic. (It only obeyed instructions in Gaelic, so I learnt the Gaelic for shut the door, *Duin and Doris* and sit down, and dinner.) Tummock gave my brother his passion for poaching, and they spent the whole holiday fishing. I don't remember what we did, do you? I remember that crazy dog all right. You'd open the gate and it would come running at you, then it would slide all the way down the hall corridor to welcome you, barking like a maniac. It was neurotic.

And we sang our way to Ballantrae, where we stayed in a wooden hut, in between two farmhouses, that looked onto a red graveyard. Remember I took my red bike to

Ballantrae? That's right. Do you remember that year we went with the Haldanes right after being in Efori Nord and Kenny Haldane got sunburn no from being in Romania but from Scotland? Bright red. Do you remember those big football matches we had on the farmer's fields in Ballantrae, and those girls from the farmhouse on the hill, who asked me if your colour was really a tan, you'd told them it was! And I told them that no, it wasn't a bloody tan! Christ that wee hut was terrific. No running water. No toilet. Remember we collected water from the tap at the farm down the hill on the left. And it had those lovely wee gas mantle lights, they'd get holes in them awful easy, they were that fragile. And we got obsessed with playing that word game password in the evenings. I used to find your hidden words in wee slips of paper inside shoes and all sorts.

Remember that time we went to Mull without your mother? And you made friends with that bunch of girls on the camping site. They made the holiday for you. They wanted to cart you everywhere. I remember they used to heat up tinned mince and tinned peas. It was unbelievably delicious, the best meal of my entire life in a plastic camping bowl; with a plastic spoon. Did I regret not coming on that holiday! I missed you all so much. I was ill. I remember you phoning from a call box in Dervaig and me sobbing down the phone. I don't remember you doing that. I do, your mother was upset. You should have come. Ah well, it's years ago now. Do you remember that other holiday in the caravan Frith Finlayson lent us in

Aviemore? Your mother was in Russia at the beginning of it. I remember I tied some string to the caravan toilet door to try and pull out your milk tooth. Remember those weans that would turn up on the step, at Christ, seven in the bloody morning, wanting to play with you and Maxie? I remember I was trying to get the gas canister to work and I stepped on your sunglasses and you were distraught. Those huge big sunglasses that covered your whole wee face? And I says, Give me a break I'm trying to sort out the gas. We'll get you more sunglasses. I remember that. I remember you on your knees frustrated, and me bawling thinking I'd never find a pair like them again. Then we went in the middle of the night to the train station at Aviemore, three in the morning, to collect your mother fresh back from Russia via Glasgow. You and Maxie got up in the middle of the night without a word of complaint. Aye. I woke you and up you both got. No bother. Your mother couldn't wait till the next day she was that desperate to see us, so she got the night train from Glasgow. I remember that because Mum brought us all these fantastic Russian toys, a pull-along wooden tortoise, some elaborate Russian dolls. Yes they were called Matryoshka, nesting dolls. And I got you a Kolobok finger-puppet set. I don't remember them. I remember the pull-along tortoise best.

It's like a whole new way to tackle the potent danger of dementia or Alzheimer's: my parents reinforce each other with memory. I imagine the stories as a kind of a fortress, that we will sit around the table as the water rises from the flooded moat around our small castle, and as long as the stories are shared, swapped, strengthened and embellished, my parents will be buttressed from the worst and live on and on, changing still, because all their past has been brought forward into their future. It is a whole new kind of account, not a cash account, but an account-account. And nobody will drown. The banks will not be ruptured. It's not so much that people drown in memories, or that the past is another country; for my parents the past is their future. Old age and illness threaten the walls of even the new extension, but they are still here, confirming again and again all the people they have ever been whilst the hands of the clock seem ever more fragile, like the seconds hand is a feather – perhaps one plucked from the bold hen that ran straight up the steps of the caravan in Avielochan and took the scraps of burnt bacon right out of my hand.

Now, when we go on family holidays, I drive and my parents sit in the back; perhaps that's when to date the strange reversal of roles that happens between parent and child. My dad still sings, and is still accompanied by my mum. It has a whole new beauty because I dread them dying. I keep trying to jostle myself out of this acute relationship to time and live in the moment, enjoy the moment, but the moment is still tinged with not a remembrance of temps perdu, but a foreboding about lost future time. I don't know if there's a word for it, but it's a feeling I'm sure many people have felt, as they wave goodbye to their ageing parents wondering which time will be the last. It's bloody morbid. Now I drive them to Mallaig or Melrose, Ballachulish or Wigtown, Ullapool or Fortrose. It's important to make the most of time, to spend as much time together as is possible. We drive, Mum, Dad, Denise, my lover, and I through Beauly, down past Drumnadrochit, Loch Ness to the left of us, through Fort Augustus, down the side of Loch Lochy, past Spean Bridge's famous war memorial that wasn't yet built when my dad was first here when he was twenty. I almost want to wave at the twenty-year-old man at Spean Bridge who has not yet met my mother, not yet become my dad, and who is here now, eighty-four years old, staring out the car window almost looking back at his much younger self. We stop near here for coffee, and my dad stays out walking. Then, back on the road, through Fort William, by the side of Loch Linnhe, past the house we hired when my son was fourteen in North Ballachulish, when I took my parents on a different family holiday, me booking the cottage and doing the cooking, then through the moody, misty, almost malevolent Glen Coe, Ben Nevis towering above the others like the bully in the family. There's where Matthew and Django climbed, and a short while after do you remember that couple went missing in the Lost Glen? my mum says in her serious, dramatic voice, low and slow in tempo. Was it after? Was it not before? my dad says. It was definitely after. If it had been before I wouldn't have let them go. The rain drives against the windscreen of the hired car and the mist seems to bubble up from the mountains like something cooked from a witch's cauldron.

Dramatic, my dad says, Christ Almighty, what a country! Stunning, my mum says, nothing like it, our ain wee country. God, it's beautiful. So many trips and journeys around Scotland involve paying it effusive compliments as if we believe the country has a large listening ear, cocked to the one side. Sometimes I imagine I can see the land blush with recognition.

Glen Coe looks sinister to me as well as beautiful and it's a strain driving through the windy, misty roads in the driving rain, and on through the lonely and grief-struck Rannoch Moor, where it looks as if strangers could be swallowed by the land whole, the swirling moorland more monstrous than the Loch Ness Monster. Aye, there's the Rannoch Moors, my dad says, nodding at them, giving them their due. He remembers all his climbs and walks with the Weekenders, Blondie, Wattie, Gerry, Toddles and the gang, some of whom would get a bit feart out in the moors. Aye! I'm serious. Some just found it creepy. Grown men! Aye! I'm telling you! A smoky chill seems to be coming off the land; we could disappear any second and never be seen again. I stop at a pub to have a wee break and my mum and dad don't want to get out of the car because it's lashing down. I order a bag of salt and vinegar crisps and a half pint of beer shandy for them and take it out to the car. They're very excited, just like I was when I was a kid and they brought me a Coke and a bag of crisps out to the car in the days when kids weren't allowed in pubs. Denise and I have a drink at the bar, and a bag of crisps too. It's probably the most grown up

I've ever felt in my life. Me in the pub and my parents sipping their shandy in the back of the car. I wouldn't want it to be any darker out there, Denise says and I agree. You're an excellent driver, she says stroking my hand and laughing, copying the line from *Rain Man*. I nod and say seriously, using my Dustin Hoffman voice, Yes, I'm an excellent driver. My dad lets me drive this car. When we get back to the car, my dad's staring at the map. Jackie, I thought we might go the more scenic route through Crianlarich, past Loch Lubnaig and Callender, but naw, I think time's getting on, we better go straight doon the side of Loch Lomond. I agree. We've been on the road for five hours already and driving through Glen Coe has shaken me up a bit. We drive down the west side of Loch Lomond, Scotland's longest loch, my dad points out to Denise, Still beautiful, but it's become awful touristy, you'd think it was our only loch the amount of attention it gets . . . It's late in the evening now, nearly nine o'clock. My dad starts singing 'The Hiking Song' and my mum joins in,

> Oh the wanderlust is on me
> and tonight I strike the trail
> And the morning sun will find me
> In the lovely Lomond Vale . . .
>
> Then swing along to a hiking song
> On the highway winding west
> Tramping highland glens and bracken bens
> To greet the Isles we love the best.

Islay, Jura, Scarba, Lunga
And the islands of the sea
Luing, Mull, Colonsay, Staffa,
Coll, Iona and Tiree,
Sgurr of Eigg and Rhum and Canna
And the Minch Waves rolling high
And the heather tinted Cuillins
Of the lovely Isle of Skye.

I drive fast down the A82 past signs for Helensburgh, where my mum and I went years ago on a mystery tour. Do you remember that day in Helensburgh? my mum asks me at the same time as I'm remembering it. Nobody does mystery tours any more. It used to be such fun, getting on a big coach and not having a clue where you were headed. I do mystery tours, I say, and my dad laughs. Good, Jackie. So you do. That was some journey home, the mystery of the moors, eh? Talk about atmospheric! Some people can't stand it. Find it too gloomy. What a country, eh? Aye, that was some mystery tour.

1988

I've found four people with my mother's name in the records at New Register House. It's fascinating how much they tell me, who married where, who was a scullery maid and who was a barman. One family of the four women comes from Nairn, so I imagine that will be her. If it is her, she was married in 1964 in Glasgow, and now has a new married name. If it is her, she would have been nearly twenty-four when she had me, which is older than I imagined. If it is her, her mother married a French Canadian and she is called Maighread Léveillée.

I manage to find Maighread Léveillée's number easily, being such an unusual surname. There's only two in Nairn, so I imagine my grandmother must be divorced. A few days later, sitting in my kitchen in Tottenham, five months pregnant, I pluck up the courage to dial. I get through right away. I ask the woman that I think might be my grandmother if her daughter is called Elizabeth Fraser. Yes, she says. Who is asking? My name is Jackie, I say. I used to work with Elizabeth; she was a nurse? Yes, she says, sounding suspicious. What age are you, dear? I'm forty, I lie. Actually I'm twenty-six, but I'm hoping I've made my voice sound older. Do you have her current address or phone number; I ask the woman who I'm now certain is my grandmother. No, I don't have it, she says. One of the girls will. I'll give you Agatha's number and you can call her. She's Elizabeth's sister. Thank you, I say. I try Agatha's number, but it's engaged. I have a strong feeling my grandmother is talking to my aunt.

When I get through to Agatha, forty minutes later, she's full of questions. How long ago did you work with Elizabeth? What kind of a nurse were you? So many questions that I realize she knows it is me and therefore knows about me, so I don't need to be secretive. Actually, I am twenty-six, I tell her. Agatha laughs, excited. I thought it was you, she says. Mam knew too. She just rang to warn me you'd ring. She said, I think Joy's been in touch. How are you? How has your life been? Oh, we've all thought about you a lot up here. You're Mam's oldest grandchild and she's often wondered if you'd ever try and find us. Elizabeth is a very nervous type. She's had a hard life. I'll write to her and tell her you've been in touch, and then I'll get her to write to you. I can't be going and giving you her address. I hope you understand, dear. It's a sensitive one. Yes, I understand, I say, liking the warmth in her voice. I'm pregnant, I say. Are you, she says. How many months? Five months, I say. And are you married? No, I'm not married, but the dad is a good friend of mine. A good friend? She laughs. Well, I suppose that's something. You look after yourself, my dear.

June 2003

Dear Jonathan,

*Thank you for your letter and the photographs.
It was lovely to see photographs of you in your
snazzy ties. I thought I'd write a little more about
myself and send you some photographs too.*

*I have published poetry and fiction for adults and
children.*

*My parents, both now in their seventies and still
living in Glasgow in the same house that I was
brought up in, are wonderful people. I am still very
close to both of them. They are both lifelong socialists
and brought me up to have an awareness of all sorts
of things: the importance of peace on earth, Free
Nelson Mandela, and that all people should be equal.
They have a good sense of humour and are kind,
interesting people. They have been hugely supportive
of my career and are always cheering me on! Next
week one of my books called* Why Don't You Stop
Talking *is getting a prize in Edinburgh from the
Scottish Arts Council so my parents will both be
coming.*

My son Matthew is fourteen and will be doing his

GCSEs next year. He plays the piano and loves basketball and is doing well at school. He's particularly good at English and History. I know you asked me on the phone why I wasn't married, but I should perhaps say that many people are not married here and it is not such an unusual thing. I myself am glad not to have a husband to have to answer to!

I have looked up the various biblical references in your letter and noticed that most of them concern the issue of re birth, being born again. I told you on the phone that I am a Christian. Perhaps I should clarify what I meant.

In the excitement of the phone call, it was difficult. I don't have a faith that I practice. I believe in fundamental Christian principles: love thy neighbour, do unto others as you would have done unto yourself, etc.

I'm quite happy with my moral and social beliefs and am a kind and good person, but I wouldn't wish to be reborn. You say that when we meet we will deliberate on the issues of rebirth. I hope that when we meet we shall get a chance to talk about you and your life. I hope that you will respect my position and not try and persuade me otherwise.

I'd love to know a little more about you. I am very excited to have found you at this stage in my life when I had thought that not possible. I'd like to know about your time in Scotland, your children, when you married, your children's names and jobs. Did you like being at Aberdeen University? Strangely enough I was there the weekend after I first spoke to you, doing a poetry reading for the Word, the university's literature festival. The first school I passed on my way to my accommodation in the Halls of Residences was School of Agriculture.

I am going to be in Abuja for a couple of days. I'm now coming to Nigeria from the 13th of September until the 21st because I have to teach in the second part of the term at Newcastle University. The British Council has programmed a series of events and readings for me. I'll write again with more precise details. I am really looking forward to meeting you. Could you write and tell me a little more about your personal life?

With every good wish and love,

Jackie

The Granite City

It is May 2003. I know Jonathan went to Aberdeen University in the sixties and studied agriculture or forestry, and the first university building that the taxi passes happens to be the School of Agriculture. The Granite City, the city where my birth parents met, is a city people either love or hate. The granite is either the colour of sparkling silver or the drab colour of porridge or fog, depending on your way of seeing it. Aberdeen is depressingly dull and grey or majestic and magical. Thomas Hardy wrote of Aberdeen:

> I looked; and thought, 'She is too gray and cold
> To wake the warm enthusiasms of old!'
> Till a voice passed: 'Behind that Granite mien
> Lurks the imposing beauty of a Queen.'

Aberdeen has its own song, its own writers and martyrs. A city can be known for its song lines as well as its sharp lines. 'The northern lights of old Aberdeen are home sweet home to me.' I like Aberdeen. Its name means between the Dee and the Don, the two rivers. I like the light coming in from the North Sea and the way that the granite really does twinkle and sparkle. It makes the vast stone seem alive, and gives the city a presence that is both ghostly and gorgeous. I like the city maybe because I'm a bit of a helpless romantic; I've come in search of my birth parents' romance! Nobody wants to have been created out of hate, or boredom, or foolishness or ignorance. I prefer to believe that I've been made out of love. I like to imagine my black father madly in love with my white mother. When I met Elizabeth for the first time she told me she'd met Jonathan in a ballroom dance hall in Aberdeen. I pictured him then, tall, handsome, sweeping her off her feet, dancing to a tango, or a rumba, waltzing into the wee small hours, and coming out into the misty, romantic fog one winter evening. I could envisage her as pale as he was dark. In my imagination, my birth parents were both beautiful. In my mind, I was conceived between the Dee and the Don, a confluence of rivers, the mouth of two rivers.

I'm in Aberdeen for the Word Festival, but my head is reeling at the coincidence of timing: finding myself in Aberdeen just after finding Jonathan. I try and imagine how the Granite City would have appeared to him, if it would have seemed cold and unfriendly, or if he'd have loved its majesty. I walk the streets of old Aberdeen trying to picture him entering and leaving the School of Agriculture. I wondered if the university would have aroused in him the same passion as it did from Iain Crichton Smith:

> Mica glittered from the white stone
> Town of the pure crystal.

I learnt Latin in your sparkling cage,
I loved your brilliant streets.

I can't quite believe I've talked to him and am going to be meeting him. I'm excited about it. His question, are you religious, nags away at me, as does his remark, 'God has intended for you to be in touch with me now, just after I've become a born again Christian,' but I try and brush all that away, and get back to the romance of it all. Elizabeth, Jonathan, the ballroom, the dancing. There are only a few details to furnish my imaginings: Elizabeth from Nairn, Jonathan from Nigeria, the dance hall, was it a dance hall or a ballroom? What would she be wearing? I dress her in a black-and-white polka-dot dress. I hang up glittering silver balls in the dance hall.

I tell my friend Liz Lochhead: 'I've found my father.' She's amazed. Her eyes fill. I tell her the story. I keep telling people the story to tell myself that it is real. That's the strange thing about being adopted: the story of your own adoption seems like the story of some stranger, or even the story of a fictional character. It's hard to make it real. The furniture of the imagination is flimsy, sometimes, not solid. No sideboard or bureau; it's more like an empty whitewashed room with a couple of white sheets on the back of plain chairs. Even when you meet your birth mother and father, you obsessively ask yourself, are you really my mother, are you really my father? The whole business of being adopted seems on the one level to be a fantastic fiction. Something about it, even to you, seems fake. Anybody could be sitting there saying they are your mother or father; you could be anybody claiming to be his or her daughter. Yes, on some level it seems fabulously made up, as attractive as an idea, as it is revolting, that this total stranger sitting next to you, should be related to you by blood. And it reminds you of what should be obvious truths, that human beings are actually related to each other, and share similar features. That ordinary fact that most people take for granted is slightly spooky and strange for an adopted person: fancy that, the same nose, same chin!

The Word Festival has put us up in university accommodation so I'm staying in a wee campus room which reminds me of the campus room I stayed in when I was a student at Stirling University. I wonder if Jonathan stayed in a room like this, or if he had digs. I phone my mum from the phone in the room – they never had phones in the rooms in my day! My mum is just back from her last holiday in Lake Garda with my dad. After this trip, they both lose confidence about travelling abroad, the hell of the airports, the steep steps up the aeroplane, the passports and the packing. It all seems a lot of stress for a good cappuccino and a view of Lake Garda; there are lochs at home and filter coffee. I say to my mum, 'I'm in Aberdeen, you'll never guess what has happened.' I tell her about coming back from a Conference and finding Jonathan by simply Googling him, how he's a tree expert, how I've spoken to him on the phone. 'No,' she says. 'No! Away!' She's wildly excited. 'That'll be right. I remember his game was forestry,' she says. 'And how bizarre that you should be in Aberdeen,' my mum points out, like the good old other half of the private investigative duo that she is. 'And to think you're going to be going to Nigeria. Do you think you'll get to meet him? Wait till I tell your dad,' my mum says. 'See you! You never know the minute. It's like a piece turning up from an old jigsaw!'

A few days after this conversation my mum phones me when my dad is out of the house. 'Jackie,' she says, 'your dad's reaction to you finding your father's been a bit peculiar.'

'In what way?' I ask her.

'He just doesn't want to talk about it. It's weird, for the first time in fifty years of married life, I've found something your dad will not talk about.'

'I hope he's not hurt,' I say.

'He's feeling protective. He's worried for you. Maybe he's even a little bit threatened?' my mum says almost triumphantly, as if at last, after all these years, she's found a small weakness in her principled husband. Although I imagine that if my mum actually asked my dad if he felt threatened, he would be reluctant to see it that way. 'But he knows you love him, as I know you love me!' my mum says.

'I do,' I say. 'But I can understand it's hard. Dad doesn't really like even thinking about me and Maxie being adopted. He sees us both so completely as his children that it's a nuisance to remember we're adopted.'

A while later, my mum calls me again to say that the

reaction of people she's told has also been very peculiar. 'Everybody's asked me an odd question. Anne said to me, "Do you mind?" and Edith said, "Don't you feel threatened?" And I said back, "Why should I feel threatened? We know we're loved. It's not about us."'

I'm doing a reading with Liz and Don Paterson in the Lemon Tree. Don lies on the floor backstage with his eyes closed and his hands behind his head, doing some sort of meditative exercise. Liz does her make-up. I'm used to travelling with Liz doing readings in all sorts of places. Tonight it feels particularly memorable because I'm in Aberdeen and I've just found my father, and soon I'm going to go to Nigeria to meet him.

Matthew, now fourteen, is with us too. He doesn't find the discovery of Jonathan the least bit interesting. I think he feels it is disloyal to his grandparents. I ask him if he would like to come to Nigeria with me and he says no, he's got a gran and a grandpa. It's kind of honourable; part of me would like to be like him, and have no curiosity at all about my birth parents, to simply say my mum and dad are my mum and dad, end of story. But the end of the story is only the beginning of another one, and to end a story before it has even begun is too difficult for me. It doesn't stop me feeling like an adulterer, though. Matthew giggles and says that on the way back to the campus accommodation the night before, Liz said to him that the room was shite, 'complete shite accommodation', he quotes and laughs. It's legitimate to swear if you're a teenager and you are quoting an adult. 'Is that what she said?' 'Yes,' he says, and repeats it again, putting on a Scottish accent, 'Complete shite accommodation.'

We're walking down the long straight Granite Mile. It's a beautiful arrow of a long street, which stretches as far as the eye can see and is as straight as a Roman road. 'I hate Aberdeen,' Liz says, frankly. 'It's a depressing city.'

'I like it,' I say.

Liz shakes her head vigorously. 'It's horrible.'

I'd like to find out what Jonathan thought of Aberdeen, how he found the other students, what the attitudes to Nigerians were like here in the sixties, if he suffered from any racism, or if people were really warm and welcoming to him. I'd like to know what he missed of home, if his mother ever sent him any parcels, if he had any brothers or sisters. I'd like to know if he was in love with my mother, if he ever thought about me. All I used to have is a tracing: his name and where he studied. Now, slowly, I think I'm starting to fill him in a little. Tiny details illuminate, like the sparkle in the stone, tiny glittery details shimmer like mica.

Slowly, it seems the statuelike figure I had in my head emerges from the stone, and he is part flesh. He's not a person that has been turned into mythical stone, but a mythical stone statue that is turning into a person before my eyes. Some people say they can't see the glitter of the granite, but today in Aberdeen walking down Union Street, I can. I can see it – no question – twinkling, glittering, dazzling, tiny diamonds in the stone. The light is in from the sea. Tonight the northern lights will dance on the water. I walk down Union Street, turn right into Market Street, then follow the esplanade round to the sea. The wind on my face, the smell of salt in the air.

The next time I'm in Aberdeen is after I've met Jonathan, May 2008. It's four and a half years since I was in Nigeria. The city is still here exactly the same as before and the granite stone listens to it all, impassive, calm, saying nothing. This time it seems that Aberdeen is a city that understands things – loneliness, depression, rejection. The stone makes no judgement. The granite hasn't changed in years, the world's largest granite structures, faceless and implacable. Now I can imagine Jonathan here in the sixties. The city would have looked more or less the same. There wouldn't have been the North Sea oil then, so the beauty of the coastline would not have been marred by the oil rigs, and the city wouldn't have been so rich. This time, there's something almost healing about being back in the same city that he studied in. I would have liked to have met him as a younger man, even just ten years younger, before he was born again and inaccessible, before he turned into a man standing behind the thin paper screen of the Bible. I would have thought that being born again carried with it the idea of a fresh chance, a new start, or a new way of returning to the old, refreshed, but it doesn't seem to mean that.

In the city of oil and stone, of northern lights, I feel something in me shift. Being back in Aberdeen makes me sympathize with Jonathan again. I can still find out where he lived. I can pick him up from where I met him that time, and take forty-seven years off him and have him back here, walking down the very old High Street, across the Quad, in front of the Linklater Hall, walking out of King's College. It is a kind of returning. Parts of him, I can still find out about. More questions: What was here when he was here? Where were his rooms? What classes did he take? Back in Aberdeen, it seems once again possible, to rebuild, brick by brick, stone by stone, my African father. Why do I want to, though? My dad's remark rings in my head, 'I don't know why our Jackie went all the way to Nigeria to meet that bampot.' My dad can't imagine why I would want to have anything more to do with my father. I should put him out of my head. I'm not sure I under-stand it myself, the strange impulse to find out more about somebody who is not the least interested in me, even if he is my father. But there it is. Perhaps it's a way of taking control of the situation. Perhaps it's a positive thing, my own elaborate way of claiming him back, or an attempt to thwart the sense of rejection. Or perhaps I'm just creepy. Maybe all writers have something creepy about them: creeping about the place trying to find out and put into words things that should be left silent as stone. Maybe it's a way of getting the imaginary parents back, rising as they do like seals and selkies from the haar of the North Sea. In the back of my head, I hear him saying in Abuja, 'Once is enough. I don't need to meet you more than once.' Perhaps my coming back here is making it twice, three times; I can meet my father in my imagination as many times as I like. Once again, I'm clutching at tiny fragments, little pieces of information. With these sparkling, fossilized facts, it's possible to build a small wall. It's possible to rediscover those elusive parents whose romantic life charms and compels: part fiction, part fact.

I go to the University's Main Reception and tell the woman through the glass hole that my father studied in Aberdeen in the sixties and that I'm interested in finding out more. She tells me to wait and dials a number. Then she tells me to follow the corridor all the way round to room X. There a young man shows me the student records on computer, but tells me they are data-protected and that he can't show me anything more or he could get into trouble. He suggests I try the University's Archives, the Special Collections. I go to the University's Archive house through a square garden and through a red door in the corner which reads Special Collections. I feel like I'm on a mission, not to find my father, since I've already found him, but to try and fill in the missing pieces. I know that if things had gone better when I met Jonathan, he might have told me stories of his student days in Aberdeen, stories I would have loved to have heard.

A kind woman brings me a huge pile of books, protected by a massive grey foam folder, like soft granite. Here's the University's Roll of Graduates 1956–1970. My heart is beating. Between Ojo Joseph Oluwatayo and Paul Newton Okaru, both other Nigerian students, is my father. The book tells me the annual expenses fee for diploma students is £75. Students working in the laboratories are required to provide themselves with suitable laboratory coats. During the course two coats may be required, approximate cost £1.15 each. These tiny details thrill me; perhaps they are the equivalent of being bounced on a knee.

Inside this Special Collections Archive the woman tells me, 'We're afraid of the pen here, and we don't like bottled water.' She gives me a pencil to write down any notes. I open the huge tomes. They smell of old books, of the past, the serious smell of learning. They tell me that the university books a student needs for a forestry diploma cost £15 for the first year. There's a late fee of £2.00. Even the class times are listed: between 10 and 11 on a Wednesday, Systematic, between 11 and 1 Practical. There's classes the younger Jonathan would have had to attend on soil science and chemistry, the chemistry of forest products, surveying, engineering, on forest botany and forest zoology. It's a three-year course, nine terms. Forestry has been taught at Aberdeen from 1908. There's a course on forest mensuration including statistics. There's a list of class prizes and certificates. A man called Hugh G. Miller is always getting the prize. I wonder if I asked Jonathan now about Hugh G. Miller if he'd remember him. I bet he would. People always remember the bright ones in a class, the ones that outclassed you. I look down the list of prizes and see that my father got the Forest Engineering (12) Prize. I've been reading the list hungrily wanting him to have got a prize. I want him to be clever. I don't quite understand why I should take such pride in his intelligence, but I do. If you believe in genetic inheritance, I suppose his brightness gives me a wee boost!

In the student yearbook, I find him listed. Each entry into the three yearbooks gives a different Nigerian address for him in Onitsha, or Ibadan. I also find that he first studied at the Commonwealth Forest Institute in Oxford. I want to find the address because I want to find his ancestral village. I wonder if he has given different addresses each time for a reason. I still want to see the village he came from, to one day visit the east of Nigeria, Igbo land. When I met Jonathan and asked him where his ancestral village was, he wouldn't tell me. Now I feel a longing to find out, and to go, whether or not Jonathan welcomes me there.

There's an article I come across in the magazine *Arbor*, Vol. 4, No. 1, 1964–1968 on controlled wind and forest protection. '. . . if trees were given Epsom salts to counteract deficiency they may finish up with wind troubles.' What a laugh – the farting trees of the forest! *Arbor* 3 has a little article whose language I find evocative. 'Get out the spade, George. Anyone who has tried to dig a soil pit in Alltcailleach Forest may have found himself, as his spade came into wrist-shattering contact with yet another gigantic boulder, examining in some detail the exact uses and achievements of soil science in its application to forestry. At best, plants can only indicate differences in soil; one must ultimately study the soil itself to find out what these differences are, what qualities distinguish a good soil, what can be done to improve a bad one. Trees, particularly the economically important conifer species, have relatively low nutrient requirements and their large roots systems are capable of extracting these nutrients from a large volume of soil.' In tree terms, I'm a conifer. I could look to the trees for guidance; a tree might make a kind father. I'm wishing that I'd learnt my trees as a child, that I could easily identify one tree from another. In an article entitled 'Pathological Headache' I read: 'Some people seem to think that all a forest pathologist has to do is walk up to a sick tree, find the fruit body of a fungus and immediately pronounce the final cause of the trouble.' The world of trees is metaphorically rich; I could stay reading in this Special Collections room for an age.

Suddenly I come across a photograph of Jonathan. Here he is, young, ardent, in the *Arbor* photograph, a member of Aberdeen University's Forestry Society Session. He is fourth along from left to right, smiling, standing with the other members. Four of the Society are also black and the rest are white. All the Society are men. They stare out and out and ahead, beyond the sea, beyond the land. They have a look on their faces that you see in some photographs, as if they are looking out beyond their years into a certain future. The look dates them, and also makes them appear ahead of their time, like pioneers. They look happy and confident.

I'm overjoyed to have found the photograph of him as a young man. When I met him in Abuja he told me he had no photographs of himself as a young man or boy because they all got lost during the Biafra War. I imagine this picture of him in the forestry magazine is one of the few that exist. When I met him, he shook his head and said, 'Biafra, Biafra, that was terrible, terrible,' and physically juddered. He said, 'It wiped us out. It took everything. All the photographic history, all the other family documents were completely lost during Biafra, everything personal.' It strikes me that it is not only me who has lost Jonathan, but that Jonathan has lost his past. Perhaps what happened during Biafra, the double blow of memory and record loss, is partly responsible for the plethora of born-again Christian groups in the east of Nigeria. I'm reminded of a bit in *Half of A Yellow Sun* where Kainene says, 'There are some things that are so unforgiveable that they make other things easily forgivable. Inside Olanna, something calcified leaped to life.'

I ask the woman in the Special Collections room if she can photocopy the photograph for me. She does. I would like to be able to post it to Jonathan, to give him back his former student self, the only photograph that exists of him as a young man.

The yearbooks, as well as giving four different addresses for Jonathan in Nigeria, note all the addresses where he stayed in Aberdeen. 30 Ashley Road in the 1959 Student Guide, and even a telephone number, 28272, and 305 Union Grove, Flat 3F in the 1960–1961 Student Guide. I've exhausted the yearbooks. Later that same day, I go to 30 Ashley Road where my father stayed in his first year of three in Aberdeen. It's a small granite stone house opposite Ashley Road Public School and the Old Friendship Farmhouse is adjacent to it on Friendship Lane. I try and imagine a young Jonathan opening the front door, or closing it, coming out into the street and getting on the bus to the university. What can the outside of a house conjure up? I continue to see if 305 Union Grove delivers anything different. There's a restaurant straight across the road with quite a fancy menu. That's at least something material and substantial. Rendezvous at Nargile. I sit outside, it is still a lovely warm May evening, and spy on the house my father used to live in, back in 1961, and for the next two of his student years. There's a little art gallery next door called the Rendezvous Gallery and in the window are some African statues. First left from here is Forest Avenue. That's the sum total of the signs, that and the fact that the name Jacqueline and the name Jonathan are on the shop lettering.

I return that night after a tasty meal of couscous and vegetables at the Nargile restaurant, and a strange evening looking at a house that my father lived in over forty years ago. There's something satisfying about having found it. There's something to be said for the trail. Perhaps it is the trail itself that is the interesting part, not the person at the end of it. At the end of the road, some-where over the rainbow, a man is standing who turns out to be my father. He is small in height, sweating, dressed in a long white dress. He is not as I imagined. He is tiny. His big booming voice cannot hide the fact that he's full of hot air.

A few days later I meet my mum and dad off the bus from Glasgow. They've come to join me for the weekend, and I'm so happy to see their smiling faces. It's a sunny day. My dad climbs down the steps of the bus first and turns to help my mum. I'm wearing a bright striped T-shirt because of the heat. My dad is delighted to see me. He puts his arm round me, and says, 'See, I told you she would be waiting here.' I walk them to the Douglas Hotel and check them in.

'Does it not get lonely staying in a hotel, Jackie?' my mum asks.

'A bit,' I say. 'I'm glad you're here.' It's the Word Festival weekend. That afternoon we go out to the university in the old town, which my mum and dad have never seen.

'I had no idea it was this attractive,' my dad says looking around the quad. 'Oh yes, you can see why people go on about Aberdeen. You can see the attraction.'

My dad goes off to hear Alasdair Gray and my mum comes to me, and we all meet afterwards and have a cup of tea sitting outside on the beautiful, lush green lawn. It makes us all feel like students. 'Can you imagine your father here?' my mum says. 'Can you see him?'

'What?' my dad says. 'What are you saying?'

'I'm saying Jonathan, her father, came here.'

'Right,' my dad says, 'right. So he did.'

May 2009. I'm invited to Aberdeen again. This time it's to Portlethen Academy, a secondary school, because they want to organize a racism-awareness day and they want a positive role model. I'm not sure I'm that, but the name of their project interests me – *Threads in the Tartan*. I like the all-inclusiveness of it. So here I am, back at the Douglas Hotel. I go out to eat on my own again and decide to treat myself. I go to the best fish restaurant and have some lovely lemon sole. Next morning a driver comes to take me out to the school. I'm on with a policewoman and a lot of the children who are performing their multicultural poems. We have to do the same speech four times to get round the whole school. The policewoman says, 'We're a big melting pot, like a pot of soup, and who doesn't like soup?' 'Me!' one child shouts out. 'Well, anyway . . . you know what I mean. We shouldnie be nasty to each other . . .' The children's poems are brilliant, and all around them is a fantastic display of art work, where each child has added their own contribution to the theme of threads in the tartan.

'It's time,' says Jess Garrett, the lovely teacher who has organized the whole project, 'that Scotland embraced being a multicultural society. It's time we changed the image of ourselves.'

It's a strange feeling, but back in Aberdeen, I feel like I've got Jonathan back, the man from my imagination. I asked at the hotel reception if they could tell me where the old dance hall was that would have been there in the sixties. I expected the young receptionist to direct me to another part of town. She said, 'It's here, it's just down below here. It was a very popular dance hall, the Douglas Ballroom in the sixties,' she said. 'People loved the sprung floor.' I couldn't believe that quite by chance I'd ended up staying above the dance hall where my birth parents met. 'If I had a penny for everyone that comes looking for where their parents met in the sixties, I'd be rich,' the hotel manager later told me. I went downstairs to the huge dance hall, now a banqueting hall, and tried to conjure them up, but an empty banqueting hall is probably one of the saddest places for romance. The floor had clearly seen so many dancing feet, but I couldn't even visualize their shoes. If my mother and father had been two characters in a novel I was making up, I could have pictured them more vividly. Down in the banqueting hall in the Douglas, the attempt at capturing them is dream-like. My birth parents are like ghosts dancing. Nothing more than illusions, dreams in my own head. I climb up the stairs stupidly disappointed; my imagination has let me down. They are so insubstantial, so lacking in flesh. They are not fleshed-out people, and though they are my flesh and blood, they are bloodless.

I leave the hotel and go out into the street. Just across from the Douglas, a young black man, in his late twenties, is running down the alley opposite, and for a shimmering moment I imagine him running all the way back to the sixties, swift, his arms and legs lifting and pushing into the past. Above, the seagulls patrol the city, barking like dogs. Today the haar is thick, and the city ghostly, full of fleeting images that fade into fog. It occurs to me that all anyone adopted really needs is a good imagination: more than genes or blood, it offers the possibility of redemption.

All you really need is to think you came from some-body good. And Jonathan is a good man, a man who has devoted his life, one way or another, to helping others, to healing people. Elizabeth, too, devoted much of her life, as a nurse, to looking after people. Both got religion in a big way. Both are very secretive. Both have something tremendously kind about them. Both of them have told their present families nothing about me. They have so much in common. They would have been made for each other.

At the airport, I think about how Jonathan would have been surprised by how long the light lasts in the summer evenings, how he would have still been able to see his own shadow, way past nine o'clock. His own shadow, late into the night, might have been a revelation. And in the winter, the snow, the snow might have reminded him of his imaginary version of Great Britain, the one he might have read in novels. The snow, lying thick on the cobbled streets of the old town; the snow gifting another light to the northern lights of old Aberdeen; the snow making the granite more glamorous, the deep romance of the snow. The winter I was born, 1961, *MAD* magazine pointed out that this was the first upside-up year – a year in which the numerals that form the year look the same when they are rotated – since 1881, and the last upside-up year until 6009. In November 1961, Elizabeth returned to Aberdeen to be with Jonathan after giving birth to me. I picture them walking up the old High Street in Old Aberdeen, near the Botanical Gardens. I picture them heading up the

Chanonry towards St Machar's Cathedral. I try and keep them walking until they fade into the distance, but they've stopped at the crossroads between the old High Street and Market Street, between fact and fiction. Maybe the crossroads is the best place to leave them, the fork in the road, or the road not taken. Traditionally, superstitiously, suicides were buried at crossroads to stop them returning and wreaking havoc on their living relatives.

I order a gin and tonic. I take a good swig. The ice in my glass melts too quickly. When the snow melts, there's nothing but slush and sludge. I don't imagine I'll be back in Aberdeen for a while. In that city, more than any other, my birth parents move in and out of reality, and back to my imagination. They are ghosts one minute, haunting the city of stone, and ordinary people the next. It is impossible to sustain them, or maintain them. I take another swig of gin. It is time to let them fend for themselves. It is time to let them go. They need to grow up, those young parents. They need to grow up because they are already old, and so am I.

1991

Tomorrow I am going to meet my mother for the first time. I'm just trying on different outfits to decide what to wear when the phone rings. Louise answers it, and says there's a woman on the phone in some distress, she thinks it is Elizabeth and it is Elizabeth. I'm not feeling up to meeting you at the moment, Elizabeth says. I'm afraid I'm going to have to cancel. I'm just not feeling strong enough. It's a hard thing for me. And I've been having family problems. Terrible family problems. I'm sorry to hear that, I say. I understand. I feel bitterly disappointed, but I can't force her to meet me. We can do it another time, maybe in the spring? Yes, thanks, she says, maybe in the spring. Later that same evening, at about half-past eleven at night, the phone rings again. It is Elizabeth. I think we should still meet tomorrow, she says, I think I'll be able. I can only manage one hour, though. One hour is fine, I say, delighted that she's changed her mind, and suddenly nervous. It'll just be nice to meet you seeing as I'm going to be in Milton Keynes anyway with my work. Yes, she says, anxiously, yes. Well then, see you tomorrow. Yes, I say. See you tomorrow, then. I'm looking forward to meeting you, I say. Goodbye for now, Elizabeth says.

Ivy Cottage, Nairn

Nairn, June 2006. Agatha, Eleanor, Edna and Sheila take me to their Aunt Phyllis's cottage, my grandmother's sister. Ivy Cottage, Nairn. It's slightly outside the centre of Nairn and opposite are yellow fields stretching for miles. It is the cottage my birth mother grew up in, and has changed little in the past fifty years. Phyllis opens the door. Though technically she's my mother's aunt, she grew up with Elizabeth as if she were her older sister. She's the one the other aunts are a little frightened of, the one who my mother said was quite bossy.

The sisters have told me to let them do the talking because they've never told Phyllis that they've kept in touch with me by letter over all the years since I first found Elizabeth when Matthew was born. 'Why didn't you say?' I ask them. Edna shrugs. 'She's got one of the ways, ken, that always makes you feel like you're doing something wrong. It makes you secretive,' she says in her soft Highland accent. I nod. The land of adoption is fertile ground for the secret; it blooms and blossoms and flourishes; everywhere you dig, there's a fresh gnarled root.

I met Elizabeth's sisters, my aunts, for the first time the

night before. Three of them had come to the Nairn Theatre to hear me read my poetry. There they were sitting in the front row; big-bosomed, friendly square-faced Highland aunts. All of them generous in size and spirit, all looking physically like my aunts. One of them in particular startled me; I was trying to think who she reminded me of when I realized it was myself. Same square jaw, same shape of eyes. I hadn't thought through how self-conscious I might feel about meeting my aunts for the first time in a theatre, just before I'm about to go on! It was strange having them as my audience, but not uncomfortable, surprisingly easy. They were so warm and friendly laughing at my silly jokes, and open and welcoming to my dear pal Ali Smith that I was on with. Nairn is a small Highland town, mainly Catholic. Close knit. My aunties have lived there all their lives.

'None of us have been anywhere,' one of them says, almost proudly.

'No, Sheila, you've been places, haven't you?' Sheila nods.

'Where have you been?' I ask her.

'I've been to Spain,' she says.

When I first arrived in Nairn, the woman organizing the Literature festival said to me on the way to the theatre, 'Now if you get any questions tonight, it'll be from an incomer.' Then she went on to tell me that in Nairn people are regarded as incomers even if they've lived there for four generations.

When I met Jonathan in Abuja, he told me Elizabeth

had taken him to Nairn, and that the smallness of the place had reminded him of his ancestral village. Did it? I remember asking him. Where is that? But he wouldn't say. I like the idea that both my birth parents come from small places: one in the Highlands of Scotland, and one in the east of Nigeria. He told me that Elizabeth had taken him to the cottage where she grew up, Ivy Cottage. It's one of those names that I've known all my life. My mum told me from when I was little: *your mother came from a cottage, an Ivy Cottage in Nairn*. Just the name *Ivy Cottage* conjures up the different images I had of it, a pretty stone cottage with thatched roof and painted yellow door.

And now I'm inside; the hall is dark and narrow, gloomy, but on the walls in the hall are spoons, tiny spoons, teaspoons from all over the world, spoons from Pakistan, from Russia, from Poland, from the Ukraine, from Hong Kong, from Kenya, Gambia, Malaya, Tobago, Sri Lanka, Sardinia, Sicily, Sierra Leone, Senegal. They are bamboozling, spoons, a spontaneity of spoons, a whole museum of spoons. I stop to admire them, almost catching a tiny version of my reflection looming in the small mirror of the spoon from Morocco.

Phyllis, in her late seventies, the collector of spoons, says, 'I'm not a great traveller. My spoons have done the travelling for me. I've never even been to Plockton or Skye. I like Nairn. I like these parts. You can't beat them.' Outside a creamy yellow light falls across the fields. It is an ale evening. I try and imagine my mother living here. Everything is on the one floor. On the left as you come in

is a tiny bedroom with two single beds in it, like the bedroom out of a fairytale. Elizabeth slept here, Edna tells
me, on that bed near the window. She was here when she
first fell pregnant. Oh that was a terrible time. It was so
hard for her. Nobody thought it right that she should keep
you. Anyway, you've been fine. I can tell those parents of
yours are lovely from the things I read.

Phyllis, the eldest aunt, still hasn't quite grasped who
I am. The others ask me if I'll take a walk outside the
cottage down the road till they've explained. 'She's no
quite got it, ken,' Agatha says. She opens the front door.
I'm relieved to get out. The cottage is tiny and I've started
to feel quite claustrophobic. I'm trying to remember if it is
the same cottage that my mum and I stopped at all those
years ago on a summer's evening. I think it might be.
Agatha had pointed down the road to an empty field. 'The
school used to be over there,' she said. 'We just had to
walk down the country road to school, but it's all been
demolished and they built that new lovely building.' I walk
towards where it used to be anyway, trying to imagine
Elizabeth's walk to school. I try and imagine the whole
thing, her coming back here pregnant with Jonathan's
baby. 'The climate wasn't right,' Edna explains. 'You see
back in the sixties, people just didn't have babies with
black men. Well, no up here at any rate.'

'Elizabeth's the only one of the family not living up
here now?' I say. 'Everyone else stayed.' They all nod,
vehemently.

I walk along the country road for some time thinking

of the aunt who said she couldn't contemplate living anywhere else. It is beautiful here in the eastern Highlands;
the light is very different from the west, painterly. It looks
more cultivated than the western Highlands, less rugged
and dramatic. Calmer, somehow, it is an altogether more
placid landscape. Is it complacent? I'm not sure. I turn
back for the cottage thinking that I've allowed enough
time for one of my mother's sisters to tell her aunt who I
really am.

When I return to the cottage, it's clear Phyllis has
been told. She can't take her eyes off me, and is friendlier,
chastened somehow. Her husband brings through a pot
of tea and a plate of chocolate digestives. She asks me
about myself. When I tell her that I travel a lot, she perks
up. 'You could collect spoons for me. Anywhere you go,
get me a spoon and post it to Nairn.'

'I will do,' I say. 'Which countries have you already
got?'

'Doesnie maiter if I've got yin already, I'd happily have
two from Uzbekistan or wherever, ken, anywhere I
havenie been, which is everywhere, like.' I tell her I'll be
going to India soon, and could get her one from Mumbai.
'Marvellous,' she says, her eyes glinting like her spoons.
'There's no many got a collection like I've got.'

'Our father was a French Canadian, and for a while our
mother took a couple of us to Canada and left the others
behind, that's why some of us are closer than others,' one
of the aunts tells me. 'But René Levéillée, our father, was

not a pleasant man, not like our grandfather. Elizabeth grew up with her grandmother and grandfather because she was left here. In a way, she was adopted too. Our grandfather was a lovely man, a man of few words, but a lot of feeling, you know the type? Elizabeth told us that when she came back from Edinburgh from having you, her grandfather was at the station to meet her. He never mentioned a word about the baby she'd just lost, but he held her close a good few minutes and patted her in the back and then took her home, back here to Ivy Cottage. He never judged her, never said a cross word. He died the year after you were born. But his wife, our grandmother, was a different story. It was her that insisted you had to be adopted.'

'That's enough,' another of the other aunts says, as if the whole conversation is suddenly getting too heavy. 'All that's in the past.'

'It's not in the past,' the first aunt says. 'Look, she's here. You know Elizabeth called you Joy? Mind you, you can understand your parents wanting to change it. We've got the picture of you as a baby here. Elizabeth gave it to us for safekeeping.'

'She did?' I say, feeling a lump of disappointment.

'Aye, well, she wouldn't have wanted any questions she couldn't answer.'

'Like I said,' says the aunt who doesn't want to talk of the past, 'some things are best left alone.'

'Only one of us got out of Nairn, and that was Elizabeth,' Eleanor pipes up. 'She kind of took against the place. Maybe she saw it as the place that made her give up her baby? You just don't know.'

'I think she liked the coloured chappies,' the other aunt says, darkly. 'She went for them. The husband she's with right now, well the one she's separated from, is coal-black you know, black as the Earl of Hine's waistcoat.' She catches my awkward look. 'You're no a' that dark,' she says, knocking my elbow, 'you could pass for Spanish or something, couldn't she, Edna?'

'What?' Edna says.

'Pass for Spanish.'

'Pass her Spanish exam, good for you, dear,' Edna says.

'No!' Eleanor says exasperated. 'Forget it.'

'Yes,' I laugh. 'Anyhow, I wouldn't want to pass for Spanish.'

'Why would you not want to pass your exam?' Edna says.

'Do you want a chocolate digestive?' Eleanor says, the one aunt that appears to have heard it all. A big grin covers her face. 'We knew we'd like you, didn't we?' she says to her sisters.

'How did you know that?' I ask them, unashamedly digging for more compliments.

'We could just tell, couldn't we? We could tell we'd like her, that she'd be one of us. There's no side to you, is there?'

'I wish we had more time,' one of the aunts says, and her eyes fill with tears.

'I know,' I say. 'But I'll be back.'

159

'Do you promise?' one of the aunties asks me. 'Promise you'll be back?' The aunties suddenly seem to want something from me, something inexplicable, and something I can't put into words exactly, not money, not gifts, something less tangible, glamour, success, fame. Things I don't feel I have myself, but they seem to think I've got close to others who have them. 'Tell me which famous writers you've met,' one aunt wants to know. 'Have you met J. K. Rowling?'

The oldest aunt takes me into the kitchen. There's a very old cooker, old wooden shelves, dark cabinets, a small table. 'This kitchen has never been modernized,' she says, almost proudly. There's an old square stone sink at the window that looks out into the small back garden. 'And the view from this window hasn't changed in years.' I nod, looking out. The whole cottage is old and dark and smells of the past, it smells musty, of things hidden and left to rot. When we get into the trendy Aunt Eleanor's snazzy car, she says, 'I dinny like it in that cottage. It gives me the creeps. It's no like they don't have enough money. It's just that they hate change.' But I'm grateful for seeing the timeless wee cottage almost exactly how it would have looked forty-seven years ago when my mother, back from Aberdeen's dance hall, lay in the bed nearest the window, pregnant with me. I imagine how lonely it must have felt, looking out into the fields and knowing that she would have to give me up. I imagine she would have had to keep telling herself that she was doing the right thing, the best thing, the right thing, the best thing, until she fell asleep at night and woke the next morning with the early light trailing across the fertile soil, and tell herself the same thing all over again.

Edna drives us back into Nairn where Agatha wants to treat us all to lunch. They've all got dressed up for this day, a Saturday. Andy, their brother, joins us, and I'm introduced to him. He doesn't speak all that much, the single brother of a group of seven sisters. I wonder what the collective noun for a group of sisters should be. I ask Andy about his work. He fixes cars. He likes cars. But he says nothing's changed much around here in years. 'Nobody goes anywhere much. I dinny ken why they all have cars here because nobody drives them any place special,' Andy says and shrugs his shoulders, like his whole life as a mechanic is meaningless because hardly anybody ever drives to Plockton or to Skye.

Later, my aunts take me to the sea front. Elizabeth, when she visits, likes to come and sit here, Edna tells me. She'll sit looking out at the sea for hours and hours. It was her favourite place when she was young too, to sit and stare at the sea.

'You've got to be careful it doesn't drive you bonkers, just sitting staring at the sea,' Sheila says. 'I mean, one wave is much the same as another.'

'No, it's peaceful, wave after wave,' her sister says.

'Bloody boring, you mean.'

I like the idea of my mother born in this Highland town on the north-east coast of Scotland looking out to the North Sea, watching the great red skies deepen and slide away into themselves, the dark come down and fold up the waves until the sea looks like a ploughed field, until the sky and the sea become one, until everything that's been remembered has been forgotten.

Later still, my aunties suddenly ask me if I'd like to visit my grandmother's grave. I nod, and they drive me there, and there it is, the grave of the grandmother who had Matthew's and my photograph on her dresser, and asked for us apparently before she died. The grandmother I never met, because Elizabeth wanted to meet me first, understandably, but then kept losing her nerve about when to meet, and by the time she finally did decide to meet me, her mother had died. 'It's a pity, you never met Maighread,' Elizabeth once said to me during one of our meetings. 'She was a fierce woman, but I wasn't very close to her, because I never grew up with her. I was close to my grandfather.' But the aunts present a different impression of their mother. 'She had a big heart; she would have defended anybody she loved. We were all that close as a family. It broke our heart when our mother died.' I stand at the graveyard of my grandmother. She sounds like somebody I would have liked. Part of me wishes I hadn't respected Elizabeth's wishes and had come up here and met her anyway. 'She so wanted to meet you,' one of the aunts says to me. 'She always used to say one day you'll be in touch. You see you were her eldest grandchild. When you rang all those years ago, she knew right away it was you, even though you pretended, didn't you, to be somebody else?'

'Yes, I pretended that I used to work with Elizabeth, that I was a fellow nurse, in case none of you knew.'

'That's right,' they chortle. 'Well, she saw through you in a second. She knew it was you on the phone. She phoned us and said, "I think that's Joy, I think Joy's just been on the phone." '

It makes me feel slightly queasy to hear them call me Joy, though of course I know it's the name on my original birth certificate. Still it feels odd to hear them say, 'Joy was on the phone.' It makes me feel like I always was somebody else after all. One of my aunts seems to appreciate that, smiles at me, and says, 'Does it sound weird for you to hear us refer to you as Joy?'

'Yes,' I say. 'It's a bit weird, but that'll be the name you had for years. It's not that easy to suddenly change a name in your head.'

'But Jackie suits you. But Joy would have suited you too. You are joyful. You're a wee bundle of joy.' I'm struck that my aunt has used the same expression Jonathan used, a bundle of joy, and by the fact that my grandmother kept our photograph on her dresser and asked for us before she died. I wish I had met her.

The milky light spills on the land. I hug each aunt goodbye. Their eyes are filled with tears. They stand waving at me till they disappear into the distance. They've known about me since I was born, and have often thought of me, and imagined me. They see me so firmly as one of them, coming as they do from a close-knit Catholic Highland family. My mother is obviously the odd one out in the family, the one who worships a strange Mormon God, and lives in England. (Living in England is probably considered strangest.)

Earlier in the day Agatha said to me, 'Isn't it hard that Elizabeth has never told her daughters about you? When our nieces come up here, we find it difficult not mentioning you. We're always worried that something will be let slip. All these years, she's been in touch with you and never told her daughters, isn't it odd? What is she frightened of?'

'The last time I saw her,' I say, 'she told me she was really thinking of telling them, that she'd been consulting her Bible and that God thought it was now time to tell.'

One aunt laughs heartily. 'That'll be right!'

'Maybe it's harder for a mother to tell her daughters that she actually had another daughter before them,' I say. 'It must be difficult.'

'It's the values of the time,' Edna says wisely. 'But nobody cares about that any more. Things have changed. She needs to keep up.'

'What are they like, Aisha and Chloe?' I ask Eleanor.

'Nice, yes, you'd like them,' Eleanor says. 'Same colour as you.'

2003

I'm driving through Manchester Airport to go and walk my dog in the woods at Quarry Bank Mill. In a couple of days' time, I'll be in one of the aeroplanes flying over my head. I'll be going to Nigeria for the first time. I'm going to meet my birth father in Abuja, a planned city, with little history, like Milton Keynes. I drive out the airport and turn right onto the road to Quarry Bank Mill. The mill is home to the most powerful waterwheel in Europe. The estate, surrounding the mill, developed in 1784, is the least altered factory colony of the Industrial Revolution.

I'm heading for the woods to the left of the old mill house. Trees are so benevolent. I've just finished learning about trees working in the Forest of Burnley, how trees compensate for each other; if one is growing a little to the east, the other will move a little to the west to make room. How trees breathe the same air and are aware of each other's company. How they complement each other's growth, how two ash trees might share a canopy of leaves.

I walk and walk amongst the old trees here, the oak and the birch and the ash and the beech, identifying them by bark and leaf. I stop at one tree, an old beech tree on the corner before the woods open out to the fields. I choose a tree with a twin trunk. It has a lovely hollow, a fairytale-shaped hollow. Tiny creatures from a story might live inside it, feeding each other minuscule mushrooms. I put a pound coin into the hollow as an offering, slipping my hand far back, into the tree's dark womb, the tree's tiny cradle; I close my eyes and make a wish. I wish that everything will go well in Nigeria. I wish that my father will like me. I wish that I'll return whole. I decide that I will come back here to Quarry Bank Mill after coming back from Nigeria. I'll come back here, and find this twin-trunked tree again, and see if the tree has saved my wish.

Newcastle

28th May 2009. I'm meeting with a student, Kachi, who has asked me to read the manuscript of his novel. I've taken so long to get back to him that I feel guilty, and so invite him to lunch. We sit in the canteen at Newcastle University and talk about corruption in the justice system in Nigeria, the subject of his novel. Torn from his father and a loving sister, the young student Zuba is imprisoned for a crime he has not committed.

I tell Kachi I'd love to know where my father's ancestral village is. 'It's so sad,' Kachi says, shaking his head, seriously. 'You have a right to know the village. It shouldn't be all that difficult to find out.'

A few hours later, I'm in my office and the phone rings. It startles me since it hardly ever rings for me there. It's Kachi. He sounds excited. 'I've found your father's village,' he says. He tells me that he Googled my father and discovered that he'd recently given a talk at an academic conference. He noticed when he read up about the conference that the subject of my father's talk had been a cure for malaria, and noticed the name *Moringa oleifera*, a herbal plant associated with curing the disease. He recognized

Moringa oleifera because his young uncle, Nwora, had given him a chapbook he'd written on the same plant. That afternoon Kachi texted his uncle saying, *Do you know where Professor O's ancestral village is*, and his uncle texted back right away, *4rm Ukpor, he's my mentor.*

Before he rang me with this news, Kachi wanted to be absolutely sure. So he double-checked. By another strange coincidence, his mother-in-law's ancestral town is also Ukpor. He rang his mother-in-law's relation. 'Do you know a Jonathan O?'

'Yes,' his mother-in-law's relation said. 'The forestry man? Yes, I know his two oldest sons, Sidney and Amadi.'

I've got the phone pressed against my ear. 'Sidney and Amadi?' I repeat.

'Yes,' Kachi says. 'Isn't it amazing?'

I can't quite take it in. The coincidences are buzzing round my room like honey bees. Kachi's own ancestral town, Oba, he tells me, is very close to my father's town in Ukpor. Practically next door to each other! Kachi hangs up and says he'll email me. I put the phone down and try and imagine these brothers: *Sidney and Amadi*. It's wonderful just to have the names! They sound cool names. They sound like the title of a film I might go and see; a black-and-white film with a great jazzy soundtrack, *Sidney and Amadi*. I wonder if they look like me, if they look like each other, if they look like Jonathan. I wonder what they do for a living.

When Kachi goes home to his flat in Newcastle that night, he looks at his uncle's monograph *Moringa Oleifera:*

A Review of its Medicinal and Other Uses. On the Acknowledgements page it says, 'I cannot thank Professor O, a great scientist and teacher, enough for his countless contributions to my work and my career.' Later, Kachi, true to his word, sends an email which details how he found my father's village. He sends the Internet links on the articles on Jonathan so that I can read them myself. I click on one. It says that my father gave an intellectually stimulating and hilarious presentation on the taxonomy of African plants at a conference in February this year. I'm pleased to read that Jonathan had made them all laugh. I read all the linked articles avidly and think about the work that my father does. I'm impressed with the years he's spent looking for a cure for malaria. I'm bowled over by his dedication and commitment to plants and taxonomy and herbal medicine. But most of all, I'm over the moon to have discovered through Kachi the name of my ancestral village. Nzagha. Nzagha. Nzagha. Nzagha in Ukpor. Kachi's email ends: 'I'm so happy, Jackie, because I believe we have found your father's village.'

One day I have a brainwave. I could ask Kachi to accompany me to my father's village! I know I wouldn't be able to make the journey on my own, but if Kachi would agree to come then at least I would get to see where my father and his father before him lived; at least I'd get a sense of the place I come from. I wouldn't get the welcome my other Nigerian friends had described on going back to the ancestral village, but at least the land might welcome me, and I might feel some connection with the place. I write to Kachi and ask him. I want him to say yes so much, I hardly dare open his email. But it is yes, it is yes, yes, yes! I feel very lucky and very blessed, as if some benign presence is watching out for me. *Moringa oleifera*: the words of the magic tree sound magic to me. I will get to visit my ancestral village after all.

2003

It is Saturday. I've just arrived in Nigeria for the very first time and tomorrow I am about to meet my father. After I unpack in the room in the Nicon Hotel, I decide to go to the bar for a drink. A couple of very dressed-up young black women join me. You shouldn't drink on your own, they say. I tell them that tomorrow I'm going to be meeting my father. And they are very excited for me. They tell me I am their sister, and we chat together for an hour, laughing and joking. After a bit one of them tells me she is having trouble with money. I give her twenty pounds and she starts sulking, saying, Is this all you have for your sister? What more have you got for your sistah?! I look to the other friend to see what she has to say. It is best to be generous. You are our sister, she says, shrugging. I give her another twenty pounds and the one who has told me to be generous says she is tired, very tired and can they come to my hotel room? My hotel room? I say, completely taken aback. Yes, they say, just to hang out. We are tired. I say, No, I don't think so, and feel a bit uncomfortable. They leave me, sulking and bad-tempered, and go and sit in another bit of the bar, where I can barely see them, skulking in the shadow. I think I must be doing something wrong. One minute they were my friends and next minute they are furious with me. A man comes and joins me, a handsome dark black man. He says, Hello, my name is Michael. I'm a banker. I won't give you Aids, what is your room number? Sorry? I say. What is your room number? I say, I'm not telling you my room number! Sorry, he says, the women you were talking to just now were call girls, I assumed you were too. Anyway never mind, we can still have a nice time together. What is your room number? I'm not telling you my room number. I've come to Nigeria to meet my father, I tell Michael. Ah, so you are Nigerian. Welcome, he says. Good luck with the meeting. Here is my business card. We should stay in touch.

I decide to go back to my room. I don't feel entirely safe. I get up from the bar to go to my room and notice the two women getting up to follow me. I run to the lift. I charge along the sixth floor to room 603, open the door as quick as I can and bolt the door behind me. I'm out of breath. There's nothing to do but to stay in this blue room, alone, and wait till the morning.

Lagos

September 24th, 2009

I've just re-found Jonathan's email address in an old file. I hadn't thought of looking there. I don't know if he'll still have the same one or if he will have changed it, or if he'll reply. There are many ifs, a positive word really, full of possibilities, chance, and luck. He might reply and say yes.

I get out my travelling notebook. In it there's the letter I drafted to Jonathan with the help of my friend Linda on the 15th of September. I never sent it because I couldn't find his address, and it was no longer on the information about him on the Internet. Now I can send it:

Dear Jonathan,

I'm in Lagos as a guest of Chimamanda Ngozi Adichie. I'm working with young Nigerian writers for the Farafina Trust. I'm planning to come to Enugu, as part of a research project I'm conducting with a student of mine, and would dearly love the opportunity to meet my siblings whether or not they know my relation to them. I'm staying at Sofitel, room 203.

In the intervening years since I last saw you, my career has been going very well and I received an MBE from the Queen for my services to literature. My son is doing a Spanish and Film degree and is currently in his third year in Mexico at the University of Guadalajara. It would be lovely to see you again. I hope life is treating you kindly and this email finds you in good health.

With love,

Jackie

September 25th, 2009

I'm not a secretive person and so the whole cloak and dagger adoption thing goes against my natural personality, which is perhaps to be too open, too trusting. I prefer openness even if I can be naive and even if I do have a tendency to be ripped off. I don't really care all that much about being ripped off. I do love a bargain; everyone loves a bargain. But I'm not one of those people who get into a fury if a poor guy at a market stall is selling me something over the odds to make a bit of money. But I digress. It's easier to digress than think about *if* for too long. What if Jonathan just doesn't bother replying? The trouble with openness is that somebody can shut the door in your face. Nobody likes a shut door in their face.

Chimamanda's friend Ike arrived last night to join us for dinner in Chimamanda's guest house. We discovered that he went to school with Jonathan's other son. So I now know for sure his third son's name. Ike says, 'He's on Facebook.' So we look him up. Me, with bated breath, and feeling that I should somehow be in a small closed room opening this window to look at the face of my brother. He got married last year. On Facebook there he is with his best man, both dressed identically in brown suits with pink shirts, as is often the custom here. He looks a lot like Jonathan, very much like him, but quite a lot lighter. When I met Jonathan six years ago, he said his third son was not yet married, and nor had he joined his church. The third son is married now.

I've been thinking more and more since I arrived in Lagos – perhaps because being so near makes it all the more frustrating – about how much I'd like to meet Jonathan's children. Since they know nothing about me, I don't feel that I have the right to say my half-brothers and sisters. I don't feel comfortable with the language, casual as it is. It would be a big word for me to say with ease, brother, and to apply it to anyone other than Maxie. I've been wondering if a man like Jonathan or a woman like Elizabeth actually has the right to keep me from their children. In the beauty parlour yesterday, Tope, the young Yoruba woman who was giving me a pedicure, asked me where I was from.

'My father's from Nigeria,' I said.

'Oh, welcome, welcome,' Tope said, reaching for the pumice to grind and polish my very swollen feet. 'So you are visiting him?'

'No,' I said, a little awkwardly. Chimamanda was across the parlour in the semi-dark. There was a power cut. Someone had been sent to a nearby hotel to fill the keg with diesel so that they could kick the generator into action. Meanwhile we were all sitting, women waiting to be made beautiful and women waiting to do their work. Three beauty-parlour workers were heavily pregnant. It was hot, since the aircon went off too. We waited in a kind of limbo, and then suddenly after a good hour, it switched back on and we all came back to life. 'No, he wasn't interested in seeing me again, because he'd kept me secret,' I told Tope.

'Oh, but you're . . . ' Tope said laughing, searching for the right word.

'I'm what?' I haven't quite caught the word.

'You're grown. You're big. You can't be a secret,' she said and laughed merrily again. This struck me with the same thud as the electricity coming back on and the lights blaring in the beauty parlour, simple and true. I am grown. How do you keep a grown woman secret? Why does a grown woman collude with being kept secret?

Last night, Chimamanda's friend Rachel joked that Facebook was maybe not the forum for me to message my brother and tell him that he has a sister. She was of course being funny and ironic. But it begged the question, do I have the right to suddenly turn up at the door, Outlook window, or wherever? Do I have the right to text, Twitter, message or ring? Do I have the right to announce myself, whatever form the announcement takes? Do I have the right to go above Jonathan's head and tell them because they have a right to know, and might like me? And I might like them? Tope put my swollen feet into very hot water and told me to be brave. She had a trolley full of implements that she was going to use on my feet. My toes, I remembered, are his toes. I chose a bright red colour, the colour of my imaginary red-dust road, and Tope painted my toenails, carefully, patiently, with a steady hand.

In the beauty parlour in Lagos, I feel myself transforming. Tomorrow, I'll go to the Balogun market and pick some African prints, and then I'll go to the tailor and maybe have a dress made and tops and trousers. Of course when I wear a dress, I always feel like I'm in drag. But even being in drag will be fun in Ukpor. The secret is mine now. I'm going to Ukpor and no one knows. I've found out which village belongs to Jonathan. I've found his ancestral home. He never told me his sons' names. Now I know three of them: Sidney, Amadi and Ikenna. I know the name of his ancestral village, Nzagha. My father, through his fondness for secrets and lies, has turned me into a private investigator! Each discovery is a small triumph. I still need to find out his daughter's name. Just before I left for Lagos this time, Denise, Carol Ann and Ella, and I Googled Sidney O. Denise managed to find a Sidney O who works for a sport charity. There was a photograph of him on the site. Carol Ann was convinced it was him and that he looked like me, but I wasn't sure. The Googling made me feel nervous again and slightly out of control.

This September I'm not passively sitting in a retro sixties-designed hotel room in Abuja, like I was in September 2003, as my father sang and clapped and prayed around me. This September I'm taking off, out on the open road, travelling from Lagos to Epe, Epe to Ore, Ore to Benin, Benin to Agbor, Agbor to Asaba, Asaba to Onitsha, Onitsha to Ukpor. I've taken matters into my own hands, and I'm going east.

Last night Chimamanda was talking of various friends of hers who had found their fathers and returned for a village welcome. 'Sometimes they even have drums beating. It's the Igbo way to welcome you in the village.' And I said, almost involuntarily, 'I'd like someone to beat the drums for me.' But immediately after that I felt foolish. How silly! Since there will be no beating drums in Nzagha, Ukpor, Anambra State, perhaps the stronger drumbeat will be my heart's. And how many people ever really get it, the welcome of the beating drum? You are lucky enough to get a wee hello and a hug and a door opening. You can't bemoan the silence of the drum, I tell myself as I fall asleep with my painted toes on my sheets in room 203 in Sofitel Moorhouse in Lagos with the sound of the aircon in the background. I wake myself up in the night with two whole sentences, but now I can't remember what they are.

2003

After I get back from Nigeria, I write to Elizabeth to tell her about meeting Jonathan and to pass on his good wishes. She writes back to me. She tells me not to be disappointed and to understand that for Jonathan and for her to some extent all of that is in the past, a long time ago. She says values were different then, and I must understand. I read my mum Elizabeth's letter on the phone. It is the longest letter I've ever had from her. My mum says that's a lovely letter. You can't say fairer than that.

Reality Britain

September, 1980. The doorbell of my flat in Abercromby Place, Stirling, rings. I'm frightened to go down the stairs to see who it is. Yesterday, a poster was put up at the university which read: 'The women's collective are an ugly bunch of degenerate bastards. Would you be seen with that Irish Catholic wog called Jackie Kay?' I was upset at being called a wog, but also irritated that they assumed I was Irish Catholic. Where did that come from? It was a British Movement poster, and there were at least thirty of them scattered round the campus of Stirling University. There were razor blades stuck to the back of them, presumably to rip the hands of anybody trying to take them down. Because I've been named on the poster, it's been taken seriously. I've been called to the dean's office; the police have been called, and they have offered me and the other named person, Alastair Cameron, my gay friend, police protection. We've said no to the protection, because we can't think how it would work. I'm back in my flat that I share with Louise and John. Louise and John are both out when the doorbell rings. I'm jumpy.

I'm so jumpy that in the coming days I'm suspicious of

everything: a parcel arrives, and I suspect it might be a bomb. It turns out to be a food hamper from a woman called Hilary Devine. I'd cleaned her house in the summer holidays in London when I'd worked for a cleaning agency called Problem. I'd cleaned for her and I'd also cleaned for the writer John Le Carré. One time, Hilary, who was severely crippled with arthritis, asked me to organize some friends to take her out. I did. She wanted to go to the police station because she believed a man was filming her secretly for blue movies. I don't think anybody really was, but I took her to the police station because she needed to be taken seriously and nobody listened to her, and lying alone and chronically disabled in her flat meant that what was going on in her head was horribly real. She told me her name had been Hilary Smith, and that she'd changed it to Hilary Devine. 'You've got style,' I told her. And she did have, though her feet were distorted and swollen with arthritis, and though her fingers were gnarled like the twisted roots of trees, and though her house was filthy with cockroaches and neglect, she had style. Her style was her imagination. 'One of these days, darling,' she'd say in her very posh accent, 'I'm going back to Paris.'

Unwrapping Hilary Devine's hamper was like unwrapping an elaborate pass the parcel from childhood. The first wrapping was thick brown paper, the second tin foil, the third newspaper. Underneath all this wrapping were some jars of chutney, jam, some packets of Bath Oliver biscuits, a box of Harrod's Earl Grey tea and a little note in very shaky writing that looked like the writing of a heart graph, which said, *Thank you for your kindness*. The food parcel that I had thought might be a bomb from the BM was perfectly timed. It made me weep with gratitude. I wondered how it had been possible for Hilary, who couldn't get out on her own, to organize such an elaborate thing. It blew me away, but thankfully not literally.

The doorbell rang again; I wasn't expecting anybody. John and Louise had both gone out and I felt a little abandoned and a lot alone. The euphoria of being at Stirling, and joining the Women's Collective and the Gay Soc, and meeting like-minded people, the excitement of being in a place where there were other black people who nodded to me with recognition – at first I didn't know what was going on, and why they nodded at me, until I caught on and liked it, *loved* it, the secret camaraderie of black people – was fizzing out and sputtering before my eyes. I suddenly felt very visible, vulnerable, the opposite of invincible. I missed home. I wanted my mum. I remember putting on my record player and playing Joan Armatrading that day for company, singing along, in a slightly self-pitying fashion to *Willow, your willow, your willow when the sun is down, shelter in a storm* . . . Here I was at university studying English Literature, eighteen years old. And in the second year this happened. The BM chucked hand grenades full of racial poison, hatred and fear around the campus, and what should have been an exciting, intellectually stimulating time suddenly morphed into a terrifying one.

I tiptoe down the stairs and unlock the door. Before the BM posters, we always left our downstairs front door open, unless we were all going out. Most friends knew just to come in and start climbing the stairs to our flat. But since the posters we'd taken to locking the door. I unlock the door and who should be standing on the doorstep but my mum. Mum! She's driven through from Glasgow with our friend Alec Clark. She cuddles me and says, 'I thought you could do with a wee bit of support, and I've brought Alec with me who knows how to tackle these things.' Tears pour down my cheeks, thankful tears. My mum, my whole life, has never let me down. She's such a trouper. They come upstairs and I make them a coffee and we discuss the best way forward.

My mum says we should hold a meeting, a public meeting, and get lecturers involved. We shouldn't be silenced by a small bunch of racists. The following Monday, Russell and Becky Dobash, who are in the Sociology Department, speak at an open meeting and so do I. I quote Angela Davis, who quoted James Baldwin, *If we know, then we must fight for your life as though it were our own . . . For if they take you in the morning, they will be coming for us that night*, and I say how important it is to speak out, and as I'm speaking, I feel it. And the feeling overtakes my fear. I will not be silenced. I will speak. The university conducts its own investigation to see who is behind the posters. At a meeting with the dean they say that they will expel anyone who incites racial hatred, but they also ask us not to tell the press. They say they don't want the university's image tarnished with fascists. They still haven't got over being labelled the hotbed of radicalism when students threw tomatoes at the Queen in 1972. I agree not to go to the press unless I am singled out again. (Though, years later, I question this decision of the dean's to cover up the BM presence at the university, and also question, aghast, my own complicity.)

My mum leaves later that afternoon with me feeling stronger, supported. She's reminded me, by coming through from Glasgow, in an instant, the minute she'd put the phone down to me, of all the times throughout my life that she has defended me. When I just started school, age six, there were three boys who used to wait at the main school gate for me. When they got me they'd wrestle me to the ground, and I'd worry that my new maroon school blazer was going to get dirty, and shove into my mouth a mixture of mud and sticks that they'd wrapped in a sweetie wrapper. 'That's what you should eat, mud, because you're from a mud hut,' they'd say and laugh. This went on for weeks. I used to dread the school bell ringing, until one day I told my mum, and she went to see the headmaster, Mr Thompson, and the headmaster brought all three boys into his office. He said, 'We don't treat our coloured friends like this.' He asked two of the boys to hold out their hands so that he could give them the belt. He told me to stay and watch so I could see them being punished. I didn't want to see them being punished, and watching them get the belt, that close up, was horrible. Victor, the ringleader, got expelled from the school.

Another time, on parents' night, my mum and dad took a teacher to task, a teacher who would relentlessly pick on me, until my dad spoke to her. I don't know what his exact words were, but they did the trick. The teacher laid off me, and became a bit wary instead. In the end that teacher was sacked herself because she broke a girl's pinkie finger by belting her so hard.

One day, I'm walking home from school with my pal Aileen. We've crossed the burn in Bishopbriggs Park and have walked up the quite steep hill, the one we sledge down in the winter snow. At the turning into Brackenbrae Avenue, just past the opening to the golf course, three kids come running up. One sings, 'Nuts oh hazelnuts, Cadbury's take them and they cover them in chocolate.' Another shouts to me, 'Whit dae ye call two darkies in a sleeping bag? Twix!' Ha Ha! Another says, 'Whit dae ye call a darkie falling from a mountain? Chocolate Drop.' Ha Ha.

I walk on with Aileen and Aileen's face flushes red. I'm not sure if she is embarrassed for me, or for them. She doesn't say anything about them, and neither do I. The thing that is the most embarrassing for me is that she has witnessed it, my friend, and that somehow has made it harder than it happening on my own. Another day, a boy and his sister are waiting for me. They run up and spit in my face and shout, 'Dirty darkie.' I tell my brother about them and he walks me home the next day. 'Just point them out tae me,' my brother says, 'and they won't mess with you again.' 'Him!' I say. 'Him!' and my brother chases the boy who spat in my face. That boy never calls me anything again. And eventually people stop; my brother carries a fierce reputation and I am protected; I'm Maxie Kay's sister.

The last time that I remember childish shouting names was during the time that *Roots* was on the television. I remember being glued to the series and loving it: Chicken George, Cassie, and Kunta Kinte, and identifying with them. I liked that they kept their sense of humour, and that humour seemed a kind of defence against racism; you can get me down, but you won't get my soul. It made me feel buoyant, the strength and bravery of those characters. So when I was walking through Bishopbriggs Park, aged about fifteen, and someone shouted, 'Kunta Kinte, Kunta Kinte,' and followed me through the park, I turned round and said, 'Why are you shouting that as an insult? Have you not been watching the programme?' And I walked on, furious and superior, head held high! This time I didn't feel that shame, that acute embarrassment, that fear. I replaced all of them with something far better: fury.

A while after the Kunta Kinte incident, I'm at the other end of the same park. I'm sixteen and have been told to go and find something to paint in the local park. A pal of mine, Sandra, and I are examining leaves carefully. It is a sunny autumn day. I love it when the art teacher sends us out to investigate. I finish my can of Coke and put it beside me to take to the bin later. A large man, big belly and grey hair, walrus moustache, who has the air of a retired colonel, approaches me and says, 'Why did you do that? Put your empty can on the ground? Don't you know we like to keep our land tidy? Where do you come from anyway? A little mud hut?' And he walks off before I have a chance to say anything to him.

Home from school that day, I tell my mum about the incident and find myself bursting into tears. 'Don't give him your tears, Jackie,' my mum says. 'I'll get angry with you if you let that kind of ignoramus upset you. He's not worth a single tear!' She's furious herself. 'I wish I'd been there. I wouldn't have missed him.' I like this expression, 'I wouldn't have missed him'; if the big guy had been a target, and she'd have thrown her dart at his big belly, I'd have applauded. 'Some people are just prejudiced,' my mum says. 'You see him again. You challenge him. Some people are just jealous of your lovely brown skin.' (Privately, I doubted this theory, but I liked the idea of it.)

As a matter of fact I do see him again, a few days later. I contemplate going up to him and giving him a piece of my mind, but I can't quite work up the nerve. I make things up in my head. 'You were very rude the other day.' Too bland. 'Have you always been a bully?' Too silly. There's nothing I can say really to answer that kind of prejudice. It is so far-reaching that I can't get to it, and I don't really want to. 'By the way I don't live in a mud hut'? No, no, no. There's nothing to say even for a voluble person like myself. Extreme racism is always going to leave me speechless. The retired colonel-in-the-park's remarks were the first time I experienced racism from an adult. It had a different feel to the Chocolate Drop racism of children. It was altogether more sinister and scary.

Every year at Christmas time, my mum and I sat down to send Christmas cards to the political prisoners in Robben Island in South Africa. 'It's not just Nelson, you know,' my mum would say, fifty-odd cards later. I used to think about apartheid as being an extreme form of racism, one that I never could imagine happening in Britain. The idea that there could be sixteen different categories of black was bewildering to me.

It is the summer of 1981. The British Movement and the National Front and other fascist groups are enjoying a surge of popularity. I am standing at the Angel tube station in London with some friends. It is the university holidays and I'm down working as a porter for Westminster Hospital. I deliver newspapers to the wards in the morning, take people to cardiology for X-rays, and occasionally wash the floor of the morgue. I take empty oxygen cylinders down to the basement, and put full ones in the shaft to be taken up to the wards. I'm the only woman porter, and the men resent me because I'm a student, and therefore not taxed, and therefore taking home more pay than them. So nobody tells me that there is a fault in the safety catch of the contraption that takes the oxygen cylinders up to the next level. One time they fall out on their way up, nearly killing me. I jump to avoid them and the impact of the oxygen cylinders hitting the ground makes the other oxygen cylinders crash around me. About thirty of them fall to the ground creating the most unholy racket. Terrifying. Imagine that: how it would look in an obituary, *Killed by an oxygen cylinder*. What a daft death that would be!

My friends have decided to come down from Scotland to visit London for the first time. I'm staying in a squat in Vauxhall with some Australian lesbians. My friends are kipping in my room, squatting in my squat. It's our first proper night out, and we are all stood at the Angel waiting on the tube. The Angel has trains come in at both sides, and the platform is in the middle. Suddenly a bunch of five guys come up and shout Wog and Darkie in my face. They've got bottles. They break them on the ground and bring them up to my face. Rowena, my friend, and the youngest of us, only sixteen, intervenes, and one of them smashes her face. Her face is pouring with blood. I shout to the people on the platform. 'Isn't anyone going to help us?' A businessman, well dressed in a smart raincoat and with a leather case, standing next to another businessman, turns to me calmly and says, 'No, we support them.' And his calm sentence is more chilling than the yobs breaking bottles on the platform. Suddenly, four guys from the other end of the platform come running when they see the blood on Rowena's face. They wrestle the ringleader to the ground and kick him. I kick him too. (The next day my feet are swollen and aching because I'd only had on canvas shoes; the guy's head must have been made of wood.)

The police eventually arrived and took statements from us and stopped the trains going through the Angel, and drove us to the end of the line to see if we could see any of them again. But we couldn't and the whole night had a surreal feeling to it. I can't now remember if they took our statements in a room at the train station, or if it was an actual police station. I was in shock. My friend's nose was not broken, just badly bashed, and the blood made it look worse than it was, but still, she had got hurt defending me, and I felt guilty about it. There she was, sixteen, and on her first trip to London from Larbert, near Stirling, and that was her first experience. The man's sentence rang through my head for days and is still in my head. 'No, we support them.' It was terrifying because if a man who looked like that could be a fascist, you could never know who might be one, the sleeper in the crowd. His very respectability, briefcase, smart coat, neatly combed hair made his 'No, we support them,' all the more unnerving. The BM guys had Union Jack T-shirts on, and were drunk, thuggish and young. These smart middle-aged men were a different sort of fascist altogether; the kind that moves amongst you, seemingly respectable, carrying a little briefcase full of capsulated poison.

I remember the intense atmosphere in London in the summer of 1981, the racial tension simmering away in the summer heat. Finally it exploded and Brixton burned. The city seemed polarized. In the hospital, I'd frequently have to wheel racist patients to have an X-ray.

One day, a dying man whose skin is very yellow, with cancer I presume, says to me, 'I'd rather one of our own took me.' I tell him there's no one else, just me, and wheel him to cardiology. There's something bizarre and deeply unsettling about being caring to a racist, but it is my job, and the poor man is dying, and I can't suddenly say who I will take to cardiology and who I won't. The irony of it all doesn't escape my twenty-year-old self. I wonder what happens to people to fill them with an irrational fear and hatred of black people. How does it start? How does it come about? How is it possible to retain it even when you are dying?

On the one level, racism fascinates me because it is so unfathomable. I learn to gauge people by the newspapers they order. Most of them order the *Sun*, some the *Mirror*, some the *Daily Mail*. Nobody in the wards I deliver to orders the *Guardian* or *The Times*. I'm dressed in uniform: navy trousers and jacket, white shirt and navy tie, white porter's coat. My boss, the chief porter, is Scottish, but says he has great admiration for Mussolini. He's prone to saying things like, 'I'm not a racist, but I think there's a lot to be said for the fascists. They know how to organize. I'm a stickler for punctuality and organization. The bloody socialists are all over the place. Their way leads to chaos.' I argue with him and he says he hired me because he could see in my face that I am intelligent. 'Intelligence is on the face, no doubt about it.' And he says he hired me because 'It would annoy the men having a woman porter.' He's the strangest man I've met. He is full of contradictions and though I dislike his views, I find myself quite liking him. Perhaps, he says everything to get a reaction, perhaps he doesn't mean any of it. I work for him as porter at Westminster Hospital for three summers in a row. If I add up the time, it amounts to nearly a year. I learn how to assemble beds, how to safely lift people, how to take people to different parts of the hospital. I become fascinated with the underworld of the hospital, the parts that nobody ever sees except the workers wearing the white overcoats.

Eventually, perhaps, over the course of your own lifetime, when you think back to different experiences of racism, all your grievances start to congregate, huddled together in dark overcoats as if they were related. The person who says, 'No, we support them,' becomes linked in your head to the person who shouts Wog and Nigger, and they gather together, like clusters or cancerous cells.

Then you can find yourself being touchy or defensive, even when someone does not mean it, or does not know that he is being offensive. At the end of the summer of 1981, I return to Stirling for the beginning of my third year at university. A friend and I decide to visit the castle, thinking that it's weird that we've never yet been. A woman at the castle says to me, 'Are you over from America, dear?' She can't hear my obviously Scottish accent because she can only see my face. If you have skin my colour, you must be a foreigner. She is not trying to be unkind, and she has no idea that her question gets asked over and over again. Where are you from, people have asked all my life. I used to just say Glasgow. Then they'd say and where are your parents from? And I used to say Glasgow and Fife, which was the truth, but not the one they were looking for. Sometimes I'd say, I'm adopted, my original father was from Nigeria, and they'd nod, with a kind of a 'That explains it' look on their face.

Once, in Stirling, somebody asked me if I wanted to visit Nigeria, and I took offence at that. Why should I want to visit Nigeria any more than any other country? I said, irritably. And when somebody asked me if I would ever trace my original parents I always said no, that I had good parents and that I wasn't interested in tracing my original parents. And the questions always annoyed me because they assumed that you weren't whole or complete, and that you never could be unless you found out the missing pieces of your jigsaw. Often people would even use that expression, don't you want to find out the missing pieces to your jigsaw? No, I'd say, not at all. I find that curious now, my defensiveness, but perhaps I felt it was being pointed out to me, in a more sophisticated manner, that I didn't belong in Scotland.

Sometimes actually it's refreshing if people just come right out with it. Once, in a pub in London, I go to sit down in this chair and a woman says, 'Ye canny sit doon in that chair, that's ma chair,' very quickly in broad Glaswegian. 'All right,' I say. 'You're from Glasgow, aren't you?' She eyeballs me quietly then says, 'Aye! How did *you* know that?' I say, 'I'm psychic. No, I'm from Glasgow myself.' And she stares at me again and says, 'You're not, are you? Ya foreign-looking bugger!'

Another time, I'm in a shop in Drymen – spelt like that but pronounced *drih-min*, but there are lots of dry men about in Drymen – and I'm trying on a top and my mum says to me, 'That colour suits you.' And this complete stranger comes up and tilts her head to the side, sympathetically, and says, 'I think that colour suits you too, dear, where are you from?' And I say, 'Glasgow.' And she says, 'Is that right? Because I've got a friend from the Dominican Republic.' My mum shakes her head as the woman leaves the shop. That's a beauty, though. *I've got a friend from the Dominican Republic,* I say to my mum, it would look good on a T-shirt. *I've got a friend from the Dominican Republic. What have you got, you sad bastard?* I told my son that story and he had a T-shirt made for me last Christmas with those words on the front and the back.

Then there's the time when I'm in Wigtown, staying in quite a posh country hotel. There's an old lady sitting in the corner of the lounge. My mum introduces me as her daughter, and the old lady says, 'Is that lady your daughter? Oh? Your daughter is *awful* tanned. Is she *that* colour *every* day?' I imagine for a moment what the world might be like if people could change colour every day. No one would know who to fight! Once, there was an article in the *Scotsman* about my book *Trumpet* with a caption next to a photograph saying 'Jackie Kay wins prize'. But the photograph was of the Scottish jazz singer Suzanne Bonnar. Suzanne is always getting mistaken for me and me her. People will often ask me if I'm the jazz singer, even though we don't look a bit alike. Our friend Kate Henry who works for the Customs and Revenue is always getting mistaken for one or the other of us. 'Alternately I'm a jazz singer and a poet,' Kate jokes. 'It's more glamorous anyway than working for the Revenue!' Kate and Suzanne always get asked where they are from too and there's the implication that they can't be from Scotland, that they don't belong here.

At school, when I was fourteen, we were given Wole Soyinka's poem 'Telephone Conversation' to study. For some reason people often asked me why the palms of my hands were not as dark as the rest of me, and whether or not my bottom was the same colour. The questions used to puzzle me, so when I read 'Telephone Conversation', I knew exactly what it meant and got the humour of it. 'Are you dark? Or very light?' The Soyinka poem suddenly appeared in my classroom and showed me some solidarity. It was a fantastic feeling.

At high school in the seventies there was a lot of talk about 'sending them home', partly provoked by a reaction to Enoch Powell's infamous Rivers of Blood speech. I remember being about to climb the stairs to my English class when my friend Sandra said she agreed that black people should all be sent home. She saw me looking very uneasy, and said, 'But not you, of course, Jackie. You're one of us.' It was one of those uncomfortable remarks when you really are at a loss for words. I felt a sneaky feeling of inclusion, that was quite nice, but uneasy.

'What about everyone else?' I asked Sandra.

'We haven't got enough room,' Sandra said, echoing one of her parents; I'm not sure which one, but it didn't sound like her worry. It reminded me of the graffiti splurged on a bus stop in Bishopbriggs when my parents adopted my brother: *Wogs go Home*. Imagine using the word Wog for a baby.

Racist words are not pretty, and there's nothing I can ever do to make me feel easy with the N word. I remember in Vienna once, I'd been invited to a European summit of poets and each country of the European Union was represented by a single poet. I was representing Great Britain. I sat at the grand banquet meal, next to a senior British diplomat. Just as I was about to take my first spoonful of see-through soup, he said, 'You know I don't actually know if I *like* your work or if I just like the contradiction that is you. Because you know that expression, don't you, there's no wogs beyond Manchester?' I felt like taking the bowl of bouillon and blanching his bald head. But I didn't. I said something like, 'No, I don't know that expression. Perhaps you have made it up?' But that was weak, and packed no powerful punch. It missed him. I went home thinking up better retorts – which is one of the problems with racism; it is always, no matter how many incidents, unexpected, and so you never have the right answer ready. It often leaves you flailing and humiliated wishing you had been quicker on your feet.

I remember visiting a school in Berlin with the poet Glyn Maxwell. The teacher said to a large group of about eighty sophisticated seventeen-year-olds, 'Those who wish to discuss homosexuality, race or adoption, go with Frau Kay into that corner. Those who want to discuss *anything else* with Mr Maxwell, go to that corner.' And of course I got two very brave seventeen-year-olds and Mr Maxwell got the other seventy-eight seventeen-year-olds. No doubt that teacher thought she was being avant-garde.

But none of these adult experiences hurt in the same way that the childhood ones did. The worst experience for me came from my best friend. We were having a row one day on the path that led into Balmuildy Primary school. I don't remember what it was about, all I remember is Fiona suddenly turning and calling me a darkie, and me stopping dead in my tracks and saying to her, 'I never thought you would call me that, other people, but not you, not you.' Fiona was instantly ashamed of herself, and said sorry, and I said, 'It's OK,' but I suddenly felt friendless and very alone. When two Chinese girls came to our school when I was eleven, Kimberley Lee and Yuk Lan Lee, I remember Kimberley's astonished and hurt face when I joined in with the others and called her Chinky. To this day, that memory shames me more than any other. You would think that I knowing what it felt like to be called names would never call anyone else names. But I did. Once. The feeling it gave me was so upsetting, I never repeated it.

My first short story was called 'Blacker and Blacker', about a young black girl who scrubbed her skin to make herself white. My brother read it and said, 'If that story is about you, it's shite, if it's not about you it's all right.' I quite liked his peculiar brand of literary criticism. 'By the way, I meant to say,' he said to me, 'you're making a complete fool of yourself going around saying you're black.'

'And you're making a fool of yourself saying you're white.'

'I didn't say I was white,' he said.

'What colour would you say you are?' I asked him.

My brother shrugged, 'Fawn?' he said, and we both collapsed laughing. My brother never identified himself as black or brown really, and so would get perplexed if ever he was flying to India or Australia when he was the one that would always get strip-searched and none of his Scottish friends ever did. He grew dreadlocks down past his waist, just through not combing his hair. I don't think he knew that the dreadlocks would come. Once he said to me, 'Every time I'm down London the Rastas are all nodding at me.'

'That's because they think you are a Rasta!' I said to him, laughing.

'Me? A Rasta? Away and boil yer heid!'

But the trouble with my brother was that every time he was strip-searched or pulled out, he felt persecuted. My brother's birth mother and father went on to marry after they gave him up for adoption. Tests were done on him as a baby to see if he had 'negro blood'. Though of course there's no such thing. I often wonder if the story of the hospital having tests done on his blood and then his parents putting him into an orphanage is a story that he carried with him, long before he ever heard it in words, if it is possible that somehow we imbue ourselves and our personalities with our own story, pre-articulation, so the story turns into a kind of inheritance.

We had an albino rabbit with pink eyes that we called Harvey and a guinea pig called Shandy. We'd had the rabbit for over seven years, and he was particularly fond of Maxie. If anyone else tried to lift him, Harvey would kick his hind legs, powerfully, and piss. But not when it was Maxie. One summer, when I was eleven and Maxie was thirteen, when my mum was in New Zealand visiting her parents, away for an absolutely interminable six weeks, someone must have come into our garden in the middle of the night. The next morning Harvey and Shandy had disappeared from their cage. Three weeks later, my brother was digging in the garden when he found Harvey. He came into the kitchen greenish-coloured, and said, 'I found Harvey. Somebody has strangled him.' We never found the guinea pig. 'If I ever find out who did this,' my brother said, raging, 'I will throw petrol on them and set them alight.'

When my brother was twenty, he drove his second-hand, but brand-new to him, Yamaha 500 to the local pub, the Briggs Bar, to celebrate. When he came out, somebody had poured petrol on his bike and set it alight. Then when he replaced that one, it was stolen, and things like that happened to him throughout his life, a ghastly cocktail of bad luck and racism. He didn't cope well with having communist parents. When he went for job interviews, he was sure that he was being discriminated against and that nobody would have him because of our dad. He hated it during election time when my dad would drive around suburban Bishopbriggs with his *Vote John Kay* posters on the green Beatle. He found it deeply embarrassing. Maxie even claimed to notice, which I didn't, that the initial registration letters of the Beatle were *KGB*. It was all too much for him. He didn't want anything that made him stand out more than he already did, I guess. If you're the only black children in the village, that is probably enough for starters, without also being communists!

When I was eighteen, a friend of mine noticed that there was going to be a meeting in London of a group called OWAAD (Organisation of Women of African and Asian Descent). I went down from Stirling, tentative at first, thinking that some people might think I was not dark enough, and also worriedly wondering if I'd meet any other lesbians. At that point I thought I was the only black lesbian in the world. The meeting was life-changing for me. There were lots of women there my colour of skin, and fifty or so of us broke away to form a new group, the BLG, the Black Lesbian Group. We met on the first Sunday of every month for years during the summer months and I'm still friends with many of the women that I met around that time: Gail, Liliane, Olivette, Ingrid, Mo, Carmelita, Claudette, Ria, Adjoa, Shaila. For the first time in my life I had black friends and black lovers. At last there were other people who had experienced similar things. Mo or Ingrid or Olivette would come and visit me in Stirling, and I'd feel suddenly supported. The BM could go to hell. I felt strong, that I'd arrived at a place where I could properly acknowledge my African heritage and be proud.

The problem was I went too far the other way, and didn't dwell on or even like being Scottish until I met the African-American poet Audre Lorde, in 1984, who told me that I could be proudly African *and* Scottish and that I should embrace both. One need not exclude the other, she said in her decisive drawl. *Uh huh*. That was startling advice to receive at the age of twenty-three, and I took it. It was a relief; I didn't need to choose.

The last time I tried to renew my passport, a man from the passport office in Liverpool phoned to interview me. He asked lots of questions, where was my father from, where was my mother from. When I asked him why he was asking all the questions, he said in his Scouse accent, 'I'm not being funny but they don't have Scottish people that look like you. It is the Italians they have up there, isn't it?'

2009

On the Federal Republic of Nigeria's Customs Service form there are two little boxes to tick for question number eight. Family trip? YES or NO. If yes, the form says, specify the number. I pause over this simple question for some time and then tick the box for NO. Under Nationality, I write Scottish. Flight number BA 75. Entry point Lagos. Departure Point Lagos.

Lagos to Ukpor via Oguta

September 27th 2009

This morning I'm all ready and keyed up for the big journey to Nzagha, Ukpor, to find my ancestral village in Anambra State. Everyone I've talked to, except Chimamanda and Kachi, has been perplexed at my desire to travel by car to Ukpor and not fly to Enugu. 'It's a long journey, at least twelve hours. Leave as early as you can, even five in the morning, you have to get there before dark.' At nightfall in Nigeria there's a kind of automatic curfew. Many people don't like going out in the dark. But I want to see how the country changes. I want to get to know how one place bleeds into another. I decide to ignore the advice and go by road. 'The roads are terrible, huge craters and gigantic potholes. Nothing is maintained in Nigeria,' so many Nigerians sadly tell me, with a regretful tone, as if they want to be proud of their country, but their country keeps letting them down. Chimamanda tells me she did the journey not that long ago and it wasn't that bad. She estimates seven hours. A friend of Chimamanda's, a businessman, offers me a secured car and a driver. 'I'd be much happier if you were flying,' he says, troubled. 'But at least let me provide the car.' 'That is a stroke of luck,' Kachi says when I tell him on the phone, 'an offer too good to refuse.'

Last night in the hotel bar, Binyavanga Wainaina, a Kenyan writer, who has also come to lead the Farafina Trust Workshop, and his doctor friend gave me plenty of unasked-for advice (always the most alarming kind) as if I was going right into the interior. 'Don't eat any market food. Your stomach won't be strong enough. Don't drink the water. Get some rehydration salts from a chemist in case you get the runs. Get some Immodium.' 'Immodium?' 'Yes, you know, medication for diarrhoea.' And so on. I haven't got any of these things with me, just some fizzy vitamin C, but I have the constitution of an ox, and am sure everyone is exaggerating. Binyavanga's doctor friend, who is also a writer, even advises me to get some bleach, called JIK, and put a tiny amount of it in the water if I have to drink it, but not too much or I'll poison myself!

Pious, our driver, a tall, thin man, with a serious face, wearing a colourful short-sleeve shirt, arrives at seven twenty and we leave Sofitel Hotel at seven fifty. He's the same driver that picked me up from the airport with Okey. It's more or less a straight road out of Lagos from Sofitel. We're not joining the motorway yet so that we can avoid the queues for churches on the Lagos–Ibadan express road. The names on our journey, Ore, Agbor, Asaba, Nnewi, excite me; for me they form a new kind of litany. I want to learn how to say them all. The two Ns of Nnewi join together into a sound that combines N with W. Kachi has checked out a hotel in Nnewi, close to Ukpor, called the Beverly Hills Hotel. He says there will be plenty of rooms there. Kachi fondly remembers the palatial grounds and swimming in the pool there when he was a young man. He's never actually stayed in the hotel, but remembers how impressed he was with the grounds. He thinks the hotel should be lovely for me. And at least we'll have air-conditioning.

The early stages of our journey are fine, apart from frequent police stops, where the police spot the Mercedes and then me, and then put their hands through the window and say, 'Weekend money please, money for the weekend! What have you got in your boot? Let me see your papers please!' Pious gets angry with them and frustrated. He's driving a secured car, a car approved of by the government. 'They can see the sign on the top of the car,' Pious says. 'They shouldn't be stopping us all the time.' (We don't give any money to the police at all, though I know that if I were travelling on my own without Pious and Kachi, I would have been fleeced by the armed police several times by now.) Kachi often gets out with Pious to talk to the police. His quiet, polite manner proves more popular with the police than Pious's indignation. There's as many churches along the road with elaborate notices about services as there are elaborate roadblocks and police checks. Strewn across the road to make us stop are huge branches from trees, old tyres, stones and rocks, all laid out erratically like a modern-art installation, except they could be death traps.

The road varies enormously: we'll be swerving slowly to miss massive deep crevices and then all of a sudden it will flatten out, and we'll speed along. ('Not so fast, please,' Kachi will say to Pious on the speedy stretches.) Then it's back to crawling and dodging. There's no rhythm to the journey, it's all stop and start. I hold on to the side of the car and wonder at the wisdom of choosing to drive. All along the road, the hawkers try and sell us water, phone cards, plantains, a bunch of bananas, half-peeled oranges, the *Sunday Punch* newspaper, little pointed packets of cashew nuts. There are even big books for sale, road maps of Lagos and English dictionaries. I roll down the window to buy some nuts and some bananas. The boy selling them runs alongside the car to get his money. Pious argues about how much he's asked for. People are more anxious not to get ripped off in Nigeria than in any place I've ever been to. My Nigerian friends have been anxious that I'm too naive with cash and that everyone will take me to the cleaners. One of the things that is said about Igbos is that they are good with money. Well, that seems to be one Igbo trait that I've missed out on!

Kachi phones his mother-in-law's relation who confirms that the Sidney O I found when I Googled is definitely my brother. I wonder if I'll be able to meet him this time, or if I'll have to wait until the next visit to Nigeria. It occurs to me that I'm thinking about when I'll be back before I've even left, and that Nigeria has started to steal a little piece of my heart. Kachi says he is Jonathan's oldest son. I'm thinking he would be the best one to get in touch with as senior brother, because everyone will have to respect what he says. Kachi says his mother-in-law wants to know what I'll have to drink. He's already excited that I'm going to be meeting his family. 'Anything,' I say.

'Do you think you'll like palm wine?' Kachi asks.

'Yes, lovely.'

'It has quite a distinctive taste.'

'I like everything.'

The country outside the car window is more green and lush than I imagined. So many banana trees and lemon trees and trees whose names I don't know, but my father would know. I would like him to be in the car with me telling me the names of the trees we are passing, the Igbo names and the Latin names, and what medicinal purposes the trees have, which tree cures which ailment. I haven't heard back from him. I imagine he might be away travelling and not checking his email. There's some great music on the radio. I check to see the number of the station – 92.3 MHz. Kachi and I pass the time making up questions to ask the old people when we get there. We've been travelling for three hours, and are making fairly good time, when our car hits a massive pothole at quite a speed. Pious curses. The car limps to the roadside and he gets out. The two tyres on the driver's side, the front and the rear, have both blown. It's quite unnerving just to look at them. Two tyres burst to smithereens, the rubber all raggedy and improbable. Now I'm definitely starting to think that maybe I should have flown to Enugu! There's a makeshift tyre shop at the roadside. A couple of young men, wearing nothing but boxer shorts, come to our rescue. They must have parked themselves near the huge hole. But they don't have the right kind of inner tube to fix our car. One of the guys jumps on a truck to take Pious up the road to the garage where he'll get a tube. I sit in the heat and wait. What if he can't find the right tube? What if he can't fix one of the tyres? What if it is fixed but not properly and rolls spinning off when Pious is speeding on a lovely stretch of smooth road? There's no point in worrying and I'm not all that worried. For some bizarre reason, the whole time I'm in Nigeria I feel protected. *I can walk through waters.* I'm just hoping we get it all sorted and get to Nnewi before it is too dark. I move position to sit with Kachi in the shade; there's a makeshift sheet tied to two poles and a couple of benches. We've got water, nuts and bananas. It is baking hot, a dusty heat. I feel very visible, visible in a way I don't want to be, and I wish I was darker. I think black skin is more beautiful than my colour of skin. I would like to be dark. I would love to be coal black, ebony black, black as my father.

It takes an hour and a half to fix both the tyres. We're back on the road, but we've lost a lot of time and we've not yet crossed the River Niger. The journey's acquired a new seriousness, and I'm tense in the back. Kachi keeps trying to amuse me and lighten me up, but I'm focused completely on the road, and the speed and the blocks. I can't imagine how Pious is managing to drive all this distance with the hassle of the endless checks and crevices without nodding off at the wheel. I'm exhausted just paying attention. For a few minutes I zone out and when I come back round I imagine I can see the outline of my Nigerian grandmother sitting next to Pious in the passenger seat. Perhaps it is her that's helped me to find my ancestral village. It's a curious feeling, maybe caused by complete exhaustion, but I swear I saw her shape for a minute.

The road up to the Niger is smooth and lovely and when we turn the corner and see the metal structure that is the Niger Bridge, something in me lifts. I feel so full of excitement just to be crossing the Niger. It's a bigger bridge than I imagined, not as big as the Forth Bridge in Scotland or the Golden Gate in California, but still impressive. It's difficult to judge the length of bridges when you are on them. There's hundreds of cars cramming and queuing as if everyone is desperate to cross over into a new life entirely. It's thrilling because the River Niger is just something I learnt about and now it has suddenly leapt into life, and is running underneath me, like it would still have been running when I was doing my geography lessons at school years ago. The River Niger, we learnt, roughly bisects Nigeria, entering from the north-west to the country's centre, then flowing due south to the Bight of Biafra. It strikes me how timeless rivers are, how placid they can be, until sometimes their banks swell and they flood as if that is their only way of expressing rage or grief.

When we travel further east out of Asaba and into Anambra, I start to feel really excited, and also, curiously, and suddenly, totally at ease. As we go further and further east, I notice the shapes of people's faces change to mirror the shape of my own. In Onitsha a sign reads ANAMBRA STATE . . . . LIGHT OF THE NATION.

The dark comes down quite suddenly in Nigeria and it is already upon us way before we arrive in Nnewi. There's a tense atmosphere in the car as Kachi looks out for the Beverly Hills Hotel. Finally, we find it up on the left and go to reception and ask for three rooms. The journey has taken thirteen hours. We are all exhausted. A young and beautiful woman at the reception says, yes they have rooms.

Kachi says, 'Can we have an Internet-ready room?'

'Yes,' she says, 'Internet-ready room.'

'Is the Internet working?' Kachi presses.

'No, it's not working,' she says.

'So it's not an Internet-ready room, then,' Kachi says.

'The room is ready for the Internet,' she says. 'The room is ready, it's just the Internet is not working.'

Kachi shakes his head in despair. 'You see what I mean?'

I get shown to a large run-down room. It seems fine though Kachi's bitterly disappointed. He imagined the rooms would be as grand as the grounds. It seems not just the adult man who is disappointed but the young man who came here to swim. 'They've even let a place like this get run down,' Kachi says.

After we've unpacked we meet downstairs in the dining room. There's no one there, just a laminated menu.

Two men come into the dining room and sit at their tables with shotguns across their chests. Kachi looks at the menu then at me and says quietly, 'Jackie, I'm not hungry, shall we go.' I realize that something is wrong and we leave. 'I can't believe that!' Kachi says when we've left. 'How can the hotel's armed guards sit in the dining room and not even take off their guns? I couldn't eat there. I was offended.' I understand I say, and try and make my stomach grumble quietly. Kachi and I share a bottle of wine and there's an old episode of *24* on the television in the bar. Tomorrow we are going to visit Nzagha in Ukpor! I can't wait! I can't believe I am finally, aged forty-seven, going to find my ancestral village. I don't mind being hungry tonight, or the fact that we've travelled for thirteen hours, or that the hotel room isn't what Kachi hoped. All that matters is Nzagha, Ukpor, tomorrow. I practise the pronunciation of Ukpor. The k and the p join together and the word goes up and then down, but I still can't get it quite right. One day I'd like to learn to speak Igbo. So far I have a few words that I can say reasonably well. The strange thing is that I can understand quite a lot of it, without ever having being taught it.

September 28th, 2009

Up early. We have an omelette in the deserted dining room, even deserted now of its armed guards, and some tea. I wonder if Nzagha is anything like the place in my head. Kachi's had directions from his mother-in-law that will take us to Ukpor, and then it's a question of finding Nzagha from there. The road to Ukpor is much more winding than I imagined, and has more tight bends than any road I've been on so far in Nigeria. It is more like a road in the Highlands of Scotland. It's very beautiful too. A big sign reads Welcome to Ukpor, Courtesy: Ukpor Students Association, University of Nigeria, Nsukka Chapter. Motto: Love, Unity and Academic Excellence. We turn left at a blue-and-white sign which reads *Christ (Ang) Church Ukpor (Aka Mount Zion City) Diocese of Nnewi.* The *Church of Nigeria (Anglican Communion) motto: Alive unto God.* Next to that is a big white banner with *OBITUARY written in red ink and, in blue, Sir Felix Okafor Burial, Venuue* (sic) *In his Compound.* Everywhere you go in Nigeria there are wordy signs telling of worship, whether it be 9 AM Worship on a Sunday, Midweek service at 5.00 PM, Solution Night on a Thursday, Bible Studies on a Friday; whether you want to go to the Victory Anglican Church or the Christ Anglican Church, the Holy Trinity Church (whose motto is also Alive Unto God) or any number of hundreds of churches in a small vicinity, you will be offered a range of thanksgiving services, outreach evangelism, anointing services, counselling hours and evensong, and services in Igbo. The signs are everywhere in capital letters. COME LET US ADORE HIM JESUS CHRIST. GENESIS COVENANT CHURCH AKABOUKWU WHERE WE WORSHIP GOD BY FAITH. There's even, I notice, a big sign advertising a

HOLY GHOST EVENING at the end of the month, and another that promises a night of bliss with Christ Embassy. I imagine the fervour of people staying up all night to worship the Almighty; sleepless and high on the energy of everyone else, I imagine the Holy Ghost nights to be buzzing with visitations.

From all these signs, I sense I am in Jonathan's neck of the woods, his territory, geographical and philosophical. We turn into a road that takes my breath away. The whole time I've been in Nigeria, I've never come across a red-dust road exactly like the one in my imagination until I come to my own village. I ask Pious to stop so that I can get out and walk on it. I take off my shoes so the red earth can touch my bare soles. It's as if my footprints were already on the road before I even got there. I walk into them, my waiting footprints. The earth is so copper warm and beautiful and the green of the long elephant grasses so lushly green they make me want to weep. I feel such a strong sense of affinity with the colours and the landscape, a strong sense of recognition. There's a feeling of liberation, and exhilaration, that at last, at last, at last I'm here. It feels a million miles away from Glasgow, from my lovely Fintry Hills, but, surprisingly, it also feels like home. I feel shy with the landscape too, like I might be meeting a new blood relation. I almost feel like talking to it and whispering sweet nothings into its listening ear. The road welcomes me; it is benevolent, warm, friendly, accepting and for now it feels enough, the red, red of it, the vivid green against it, the long and winding red-dust road. It doesn't matter now that my father turned out to be the Wizard of Oz, a smaller man than the one in my head, and a frightened man at that. What matters is that I've found my village. Matthew had asked me how I could feel anything for a place without the people, and I'd wondered whether I might feel nothing. But I feel overwhelmed just to be here.

A woman is walking up the road with a small baby on her back, wrapped into her back in cloth, so that they appear as one. 'Biko,' Kachi says, please, 'Professor O's house?' The woman replies in Igbo saying it is straight ahead and on the left. We drive on, and pass one left turn, but Pious and Kachi are sure she meant the next one. 'I don't think so,' I say. 'I think it is there. I think we need to go there.' And we do, and it leads us to my father's compound. You are not really supposed to go snooping around people's compounds, so I feel a little wary; we might get caught and shouted at, as if I'm doing something wrong. Nobody stops us when we open the gate. Next to the gate is a sign which reads Barbing Saloon Here. We follow the houses in the compound round till we see a woman in the distance holding a very tiny baby. 'Which one is Prof. O's house?' Kachi asks. 'That one,' she points. 'The one next to it is Sidney's. Jonathan was here yesterday. You just missed him.' I'm disappointed to have just missed him. The woman is Jonathan's cousin. I don't tell her who I am, though I talk to her about babies. She tells me her baby came out very quickly, and laughs at my accent. 'Kedu,' I say, and she giggles madly, and says, 'Odimma,' it is well. Just beyond her house is the bush, banana trees, plantain trees, cassava, all densely planted. I want to run into it and get lost. There are goats and chickens and puppy dogs running around the compound. There are lizards and geckos darting about too, the biggest lizards I've seen with fat red tails. We ask Jonathan's cousin for his phone number and she gives it to us and tells us of his new office address in Enugu. I'm still thinking that we might drop by his office to say hello. I'm still thinking he hasn't received the email. I give her some money for the tiny baby and she is delighted. 'Daalu,' she says, thank you. I go and stare into the windows and through the shutters of Jonathan's house. I can't see much. I stand outside the mustard-painted front door and try and peer through the little bit of window the shutter doesn't cover. But it's dark in there, and I can't see anything at all. Then I go back to the car and start to cry. Kachi and Pious are distraught, but I can't stop crying. It is all wrong. It feels all wrong. Nobody knows me. There's nobody to welcome me. In Igbo the word for welcome is 'nno'.

We drive into Ukpor. There's a big market at Ukpor, bustling and vivid. A row of five striking-looking Igbo women show me their wares, lovely printed cloths. I decide to buy one as a memento even though I already bought lots of cloth at Balogun market in Lagos. Quite a crowd gather round me in the market. They are shouting, 'Oyibo!' At first I'm delighted because I think they are saying Igbo! I think they are recognizing me as a fellow

Igbo. Then Kachi says, 'No, they are saying Oyibo; it's a pidgin word for white person.'

'Oh, I see,' I say, deflated. 'White person?'

'Yes,' Kachi says, 'O-y-i-bo. Some are saying "Onye ocha", also another word for white person.' So you have come back to Nigeria and brought your white wife is what people are saying to Kachi, admiringly. No, Kachi tries to explain, she is not my wife and she is not white. Kachi's embarrassed, perhaps a little bemused. And certainly a lot anxious about the amount of attention I'm attracting. It's impossible, it seems, to keep a low profile with skin as light as mine in Ukpor market.

I spent some of my childhood wishing I was white like the other kids and feeling like I stuck out in Scotland like a sore thumb; and now, in Nigeria, I'm wishing I was black, and feeling like I stick out like a sore thumb. It's the first time in my life that I've properly understood what it means being mixed race. It's not a term I've ever embraced, and I've always felt more black than white; but now here suddenly in Nigeria, people are following me around Ukpor market and touching my skin and saying *Oyibo* and *Onye ocha!* I realize I want to be accepted. I want other Nigerians to see in my face that my father is Igbo. In Lagos, there was nothing like this, it being a big city, I felt like I blended in there. The women in the stall at Ukpor are enchanted with me, fat and middle-aged though I am, just because of my light skin. I start to really dislike it. I want to sit out in the broad bold sun for hours till my skin fucking toughens up.

Kachi has other worries. He worries that I'm drawing too much attention to myself; everyone is crowding round me in the teaming market selling cloths and foods and fruits and everything you could need or imagine. This is Anambra State and in this last year alone there have been six hundred and fifty kidnappings. 'Don't worry,' I say to Kachi. 'I'm not going to get kidnapped.' Though the idea intrigues me, whether I'd be one of those people that would develop a close relationship with their kidnapper or not. I say this to Kachi – 'Don't, Jackie, please, don't joke.' Kachi's mother-in-law phones him every day to check that all is well with us. I hadn't realized before we came here that I would be such a worry and responsibility.

The next day we go to Oguta to meet the oldest man, Udom Ogene, and the oldest woman in town. Ogene is the generic name in Oguta for the oldest person in the village. I want to talk to old Igbo people about their customs and beliefs and how they've changed over their lifetime; and then to do the same in the Scottish Highlands and Islands. It interests me that my father is from a village in eastern Nigeria and my mother from a small town in the eastern Highlands of Scotland. I'm inspired by writers like Hugh Miller and Studs Terkel to try and collect these oral stories together. The Nigerian writer Flora Nwapa came from Oguta. I'm trying to remember the name of the book of hers that I loved years ago and reviewed for *Spare Rib* back in the eighties. *Efuru*, that was it. I'll need to return to it now that I've been to Oguta. How our lives are mapped by books.

It takes the Udom Ogene a long time before he comes out and lies on the dilapidated sunbed on his veranda. He has worked out that he is roughly one hundred and thirteen years old, though I'm not sure if he is *that old*, but he definitely is very, very old. He is wearing a red woollen hat with a pom-pom to denote that he is the Ogene, with a feather stuck in it too, and a blue necklace around his neck. He wears on his wrist a staff, which his father had worn before him. Before we can start talking, we have to be blessed – the kola nuts first. Then the old man blesses me with the clay dust from the river. I kneel down in front of him and he sprinkles it on my hair. My knees hurt having to bend so much, but hopefully it will be worth it. He is serious in his blessing, and the intensity of it, the belief that he has in his own powers, remind me of my father. He speaks long sentences in Igbo and after each everyone present says, 'Ise.' Amen. I join in and say Ise in the same incantatory way. I like it! Issaaaaay, the emphasis is on the end, the ay sound and the ay rises, and rises, till it sounds like a word being lifted up to the bright blue sky. He says the blessing is a mighty business and it has to be taken seriously; at the end of the long blessing, I do feel blessed.

The old man tells me he wouldn't have come out if the spirits had told him we weren't good people. He says he sees a lot of spirits these days; they come to join him often. The older he has become the more spirits he sees so he spends most of his time in the spirit world. He says he prays to his idols and that counts for his god. He says many men go to church and pray to a god and then do bad things, but he prays to his idol and has always been a good man. 'I've been alive a very long time,' the oldest man in Oguta says. In the past, people were punished and thrown into the evil forest; their bodies would not be buried if they had committed an abomination or committed suicide. The old man has taken a liking to me. He said he was born with his disability, a crooked foot, but that other than that he is well. He puts it down to drinking the water from the river every day. The steps up to his house are huge boulders, uneven and difficult; I found it hard to climb up there. But he is strong and manages them and has no problem about taking his bath in the river near his house.

Then we go to visit the oldest woman, Nwanyiafor Oshiekwe, who is also wearing a knitted red hat with a pom-pom. She is one hundred and nine, she says. She, too, blesses me with kola nuts before we begin. She has never had children though she married a woman (an Igbo custom) so that she could also be her husband's other wife, and that wife had children. She was never jealous of her, she says, they were all just one family. At celebrations, she danced, she says, her eyes alive and twinkling with the memory of her girl self. She starts to dance for me in her chair. Later, she blesses me again when I ask if I might have some of the local gin, sitting on the table, some *kai kai*. She's delighted. She pours a little gin on the ground. She blesses theatrically and everyone says Ise again, Amen, Amen. I throw some of the hot white lightning down my throat. Very good, I tell her, and she's bemused. Then she tells me the gin comes from Ukpor – it's my hometown gin!

We all decide to go out on a boat on Lake Oguta, where there are two townships separated by the lake, the second-largest freshwater lake in Nigeria. The boat takes us out to the place where Lake Oguta meets the Urashi River, and I can see the different colours of the waters, the natural confluence, brown and blue, and how they don't mix, like two silent sides of a family feud, like the Dee and the Don.

Later, we check into Naija Plaza Hotel, where a big television is showing a match between Arsenal and a Greek team. When Arsenal scores, Pious shouts out, 'Fantastic!' and a man across the bar shouts 'Fantastic!' too. The hotel has fast green geckos crawling across the bedroom walls with their specialized toepads and lack of eyelids. When the power goes, I'm engrossed in a Nollywood film about jealousy and love. I find myself sitting in the dark for the longest time, wondering if I should crawl to my mobile phone to get some light. Just when I'm thinking that the dark isn't all that unpleasant unless a gecko crawls across my face, the light comes back on. I catch up with the Nollywood. It's great just to see so many black faces on the television even if the acting isn't brilliant and the storylines are hackneyed. Nollywood makes me know I'm in Nigeria as much as wandering through the market at Ukpor. Tomorrow we're going back to Nzagha. I feel like I'm getting ready to meet a lover; it is after all possible to feel love for the land.

We drive along Nnewi New Road, Oba. 'We are good people living in a great Nation, Nigeria,' the radio blares. Tomorrow is the 49th Independence Day from the British. Oguta, where we've just come from, was one of the first territories used by the British to advance into the Igbo hinterland. We come into Nnewi and there's a view of a massive pile of refuse on the hill. Pious sucks his teeth. 'Independence and they can't even sort out this rubbish!'

Then we branch off left. 'Stuck on you,' Lionel Ritchie sings on the car radio, 'I've got this feeling deep down in my soul that I just can't lose / Guess I'm on my way . . . Mighty glad you stayed.' I've decided, for now, decisions being tenuous and open to change, that I will drop by Jonathan's office tomorrow with Kachi and see if I can see him. I hope he will be in. 'Been a fool too long guess it's time for me to come on home.' Today the red of the road is even richer because it has rained, and it is not dusty any more. There are mango trees and guava trees and pawpaw trees. There are cassava and yam farms and elephant grasses. We pass some lemon trees and another huge mansion. The *ixora* flowers are blooming. A woman appears from nowhere on a motorbike. She drives past me, and then turns round and passes us again. I have a strange feeling she might be my sister.

It was odd getting to Nzagha yesterday to discover that my father had just left the day before. If he is not in his office today in Enugu, so be it, or if he is in and doesn't want to see me, so be it. But I'll make sure Kachi stays with me. I don't want to go through the Nicon Hotel experience twice. I try and think what I'd like best, what the best possible outcome could be. What I'd really like would be for Jonathan to say, 'I will tell my children and one day we will all welcome you to the village; one day you will return here to the sound of the drums.' Or, what I would like would be for Jonathan to say, 'I'm sorry, I know this is wrong, but I can't do anything else, but you can tell my children if you like.' Or for him to say, 'I will find a way for you to meet them if you agree not to tell them who you really are.' But I'm not so certain how I'd manage that if it came to it. It would upset me like it upset me yesterday seeing his cousin holding her three-week-old baby and not feeling able to say to her, 'I'm Jonathan O's daughter.'

I asked each of the people I talked to today, if an Igbo man had a child a long time ago and the child returned what would he do, and all of them, categorically and without exception, said that he would acknowledge the child. I asked the oldest woman in Oguta who said, when I pressed her about it and said, 'What if a man didn't acknowledge his child', 'It is not possible. It is his blood. It is not possible for an Igbo man not to acknowledge his blood.' Which reminded me of Jonathan's exact phrasing from that time, and I'd found it curious, 'I have come here on the bus from Enugu. I have acknowledged you.' In his mind, he had already done what an Igbo man should do. One thing I did think travelling the long road to Ukpor from Lagos was that Jonathan's bus trip to meet me was no small thing: those roads, those miles, those potholes, those police checks. He went through them all, eight hours on a hot and overcrowded small bus, to come and meet me. No small thing. Perhaps, I should see that journey of his through new eyes, now that I know what such a journey entails and how *gruelling* (Kachi's word to his cousin about our journey) such a journey can be. Like Jonathan said in Abuja, 'I have come to meet you. I have travelled all this way to meet you in my spiritual home which is Abuja.' Whether he agrees to see me again or not, at least he did come that once.

This time we don't go into Jonathan's compound. I daren't risk looking inside Jonathan's house again, or staring at Sidney's twin bungalow. Anyway, the feeling of being in the compound without actually being invited by Jonathan was disquieting. It made me feel a bit like a private eye in what could have been my own life, spying on my other self. I think of 'The Road Not Taken'. I say the poem off by heart silently to myself. *Two roads diverged in a yellow wood, / And sorry I could not travel both / And be one traveller, long I stood / And looked down one as far as I could / To where it bent in the undergrowth; / Then took the other . . .* 'Yesterday we were extraordinarily lucky,' Kachi says, 'that Jonathan's cousin allowed us to walk around the compound. Today she might be suspicious.' I look at the gate to the compound from afar and wonder whether I might ever actually go through it as an invited person, and how wonderful that would feel. Driving back past the sign that says *Holy Ghost Mercy Specialist Hospital*, past the Ubu stream, the radio plays 'Nothing compares to You'. Nothing compares, nothing compares . . . to you. When I see the sign that reads GOODBYE FROM UKPOR, I reply to it out loud: *Goodbye, Ukpor, goodbye.*

2009

Okey, Chimamanda's brother, meets me at Lagos International Airport. A porter called Peter helps me out with my bags and then writes his telephone numbers on the customs service form that I've filled in wrongly. Please, I would like to see you again, Peter says.

The last time I was in Nigeria, on the way to Kano from Abuja with the British Council, a baggage man at the airport said, That will be five hundred naira, your case is too heavy. Excess, please! Then the man next to him said, And what have you got for your brother, since you gave money to that brother. So I gave him five hundred naira. And then a third man said, And what have you got for your brother since you gave those two brothers money. And I gave him five hundred naira also. The British Council man came running up and argued with the men and they handed me the money back. Then the first one said, And what have you got for your brother for giving you the money back. I laughed. I gave him the five hundred naira again. And the second one said, And what have you got for your brother for giving you the money back. And I gave him five hundred naira. And the third one just held out his hand and I put the five hundred in it. The man from the British Council shook his head in despair.

I tell Okey this story and we laugh all the way to the hotel. It's great being back in Nigeria, and this time it feels very different from the last. I'm here under my own steam. The second day I run a workshop for the Farafina Trust, organized by Chimamanda. I ask the writers to tell me their names and a story about the meaning of their names. Pelu, an elegant dark black man, with kind, twinkling eyes, a travel writer, tells me his name means 'another brave person has been added to the family'. Ikeogu, a handsome round-faced man, who has been writing a long opera since the fatwa was announced on Salman Rushdie, says every line of my work can be sung, it's all iambic pentameters, and starts to sing it, tells me his name means 'mighty in battle'. Jekwu, a flamboyantly dressed man with a high-pitched voice and a brilliant imagination, tells me his name means 'it is left for God to decide'. Martina who has come from Ghana says her name means 'fish from the sea'. Amanda says her name means 'so many stories to tell'.

I want to hear all of the stories, the stories of Wunji, Tunje, of Fumi, Oyinda, Naomi and Onyinye. Tonight at dinner, Chimamanda's friend Louis tells a story about how he had to eat yam porridge during the war and has never liked it since. Later, Louis drives me back to the hotel; Ray Charles is singing 'Hit the Road, Jack'.

Glasgow Royal Infirmary

April 17th, 1978 is one of the few dates I can remember accurately because it is the day I broke my tibia and fibula in my left leg. It was a lovely spring evening; the pink blossom frilled the branches of the cherry tree that my parents planted when they brought my brother back from the orphanage. I decided I would take a ride on the Honda 50 moped I'd bought with the money my grand-mother had left me, money she'd earned cleaning the houses of well-to-do Glaswegians, and then come back and swot up on World War One. The O-level examina-tions had already started, bringing with them that strange mixture of extra time from study periods and extra pres-sure. But I love revision. I'd made myself a very elaborate timetable using different coloured markers. I decided that instead of settling right down to the revision after school, I would take a ride on my moped. I was driving confi-dently towards Kirkintilloch when I decided I would take a turn-off to Lenzie that I'd never taken before. And that spontaneous decision changed my life. I was singing a Billy Ocean song, 'Love Really Hurts Without You', though I wasn't thinking about anybody in particular. I looked behind me to check it was safe to change lanes, I'd looked in front and no one else was turning right. When I looked back up there was a car suddenly stopped in front of me, not indicating. I swerved to try and miss it. Then, according to eyewitnesses, I was thrown into the air. I hit another car coming towards me and then flew over the roof of a third car and rolled and rolled and rolled and landed outside a graveyard. (My mum said later, it was handy and they could have just thrown me over the wall.) I remember the sensation of rolling through the air, it seemed to take place in slow motion, and be almost dreamy. At some point I stopped and there were suddenly people around me. It occurred to me that I might actually be dead, since I couldn't speak or shout, but my thoughts were still going on. What if this is what death is like? I remember wondering. What if they put you in the ground and your thoughts continue? I felt as if I was outside myself looking down, and as if I had split into two.

A man is holding my leg in his hands. It feels like he is squeezing it. 'You're going to be all right,' he says. 'The ambulance is on its way.' I can hear him. His voice comes though I can't see his face properly just yet. Maybe that means I am alive. Can you hear things when you are dead? Maybe the dead hear all sorts. People on a double-decker bus are looking down at me from the top window as I am lying on the road looking up at them. They seem to be staring for ages. The bus is just stopped there in the middle of the road. There must be a traffic jam. (It takes me ages, looking back on this accident scene with me lying in the middle of the road, to realize that I am the jam. I am the traffic jam, and my blood is the jam on the road.) I wish they'd look the other way. I ask the man with the bald head and the anxious face to stop squeezing my leg. 'I'm not,' he says. 'I'm just trying to hold it. It's the pain.' Finally, it seems like ages, and it is apparently half an hour, an ambulance arrives. First of all they deal with the woman whose car I hit. She's in shock. It turns out she's an English teacher at my school and knows me. They give her something for her shock. Then they get me into the ambulance. A man is in there already in a terrible state. His face is burnt with tar macadam. The ambulance men put my leg into a plastic balloon thing, it's a plastic splint and it is agony. They tell me it's a compound fracture and the bone has broken through the skin. They tell me it'll keep my bone in place before the operation. The man with the burnt face makes jokes all the way to the hospital, though he must be in terrible pain. When we arrive at Glasgow Royal Infirmary, the ambulance men want to get him out first, but he says, 'No, after this young motorbike rider!' He tells me to take care and I tell him the same – injured soldiers that we are. He's made me brave.

It seems ages lying on a hospital trolley before I hear in a room next door the far away voice of my mum. I start shouting for her. 'Mum! Mum!' The nurse comes charging in and tells me if I don't pipe down I won't be getting to see my mother. My mum rushes through. She's trying to be calm, though I can see she wants to be sick. My brother's with her all worked up and my best friend Alastair. My brother says, 'You should see the state of your face, Jacks, scarred for life, I'd say. Yip, scarred for life, I reckon.'

'Get me a mirror,' I whisper. I stare into the mirror; my face looks a bloody mess.

'The face heals quickly,' my mum says, giving my brother a look.

Then he says, 'Can I have your helmet, it's still in no bad condition considering?' The yellow helmet is bizarrely in the room on a chair, sitting there all innocent and knowing. There's a bag of bloodied clothes there too, my pink cords that had to be cut off me soaked in blood and my lime-green quilted Chinese jacket. I'd felt quite springlike when I'd left my house dressed in the colours of lime and cherry blossom.

My mum told me a few weeks later that she'd been given the bag of bloodied clothes to take home, and that when she got in and opened them up she vomited. 'It's when it properly hit me,' she said, 'only when I got home. That you could have died.'

In the hospital emergency ward, my mum holds my hand and repeats like a mantra, 'You're being a brick, Jackie, you're such a brick.'

'I'm thirsty, can you get me some water?'

My mum pours a plastic cup of water from the sink in the corner of the strange room we're in, and the nurse comes in just as she is about to give it to me.

'She can't have that!' she barks. 'She's going to be operated on in a few hours. No liquids.'

'She's terribly thirsty,' my mum says.

'Wet her lips, no more than that!' the nurse says sternly.

My mum dips her fingers into the cup and traces round the edges of my lips.

'Can I have this helmet?' my brother asks again.

'For goodness' sake, Maxwell,' my mum says impatiently. 'Go home. You're not helping anybody.'

My brother slams out of the emergency ward, annoyed, and my mum raises her eyebrows.

My mum goes and so does my friend Alastair, who stays the night at my house to comfort my mum. When she gets home, my mum calls my dad, who is at the Trade Union Conference in Aberdeen. She says, 'John, there's been an accident, Jackie's got a compound fracture in her leg.' But my dad, who has had a drink because there's been a social, hears her say, 'Jackie's got a compound fracture in her head,' and puts down the phone and goes off to the toilet to throw up.

They operate on me at one in the morning. When I wake hours later dying of thirst, I'm allowed to drink. It feels as if there's a huge fire inside my leg. I have a full-length plaster on it that stays on for the next sixteen weeks, followed by a plastic splint for the next six months with a walking stick. It's a year and a half before I walk properly again, and I never run again, not like I used to run, because I used to run for the Scottish School Girl County Championships, doing the four-mile cross-country run, and I used to train five days a week, practising hill starts on the steep Boclair Road with my PE teacher Mrs Fife shouting instructions. I liked long distance and I liked sprinting. I liked the free fast feeling when your arms powered your body, the exhilaration of it. At one point in my life, I thought that would be what I do, run and run and run. The bone never quite heals and I'm left with a leg that is half an inch shorter than the other, which gives me a wee limp when I'm tired.

A couple of days later a big bouquet of flowers arrives from my dad and other trade unionists in Aberdeen. When my mum comes to visit me the next night in hospital, I say to her look at my lovely buffet, and she laughs and laughs. 'Bouquet,' she says. 'Buffet's what we prepare for our socials. Wait till I tell your dad.'

The hospital days are long and slow. I get to know all the characters in my ward, and how to use my crutches and hobble to the television room. A tall old woman with white hair and a sling round her left arm looks at my full-length plaster with envy. 'Ah,' she says, 'you're a leg. I'm an arm. The legs get all the sympathy.' We watch an episode of *Z Cars* together, but I find myself feeling jangled with the sound of sirens. The world suddenly seems more vulnerable; nothing can be predicted, not even your O-levels – which the spell check has just decided should read olives. Yes, true, nothing can be predicted, not even your olives. The road less travelled by can lead to death at seventeen before you have even learnt that love was made for beauty queens.

Another old woman in the corner bed in our orthopaedic ward has just been told that she can go home on Saturday, same day as me. She doesn't look happy. 'Are you not pleased you're going home?' I ask her later.

'No,' she tells me. 'It's better in here. Hospital is better than home. There's more company, dear.' A little tear rolls down her cheek and settles in a ridge made from a wrinkle. 'The spring is here but I'm no spring chicken,' she says to me and tries to chortle a little. 'You're a good listener for a girl your age,' she says. I worry about her. Then I worry about the woman in the bed next to her, who is very silent and troubled. I find myself worrying about the whole ward, and feeling lucky that I have a mum and dad and a brother to go home to, lucky that I am alive.

In the next few weeks I think about death a lot. Getting close to death, it seems to whisper at the edge of your cheek. Nearly dying brings you closer to living. There's a thin border; you feel yourself cross it, going back to the land of the living, going home. Perhaps, if you'd gone the other way, death would have been a different home.

My dad comes back from the conference on the day I'm allowed home from hospital. He comes to pick me up. I'm not yet brilliant with the crutches and find the thirteen stairs in my house a nightmare. My dad gets himself all worked up into a state of high anxiety, shouting at me on the stairs, 'Come on, come on, for Christ sake!'

My pal Alastair is behind me speaking in a soft voice and my mum is at the top of the stairs saying quietly, 'You can do it. John, stop shouting, you're not helping her.' Finally I make it to my bedroom and lie down with my big hard white leg elevated. It feels so itchy. I want to get a knitting needle and push it down the hole in the top.

The nights are long and hot and uncomfortable with a full-length plaster on your leg. You try and sleep on your back and that doesn't work and then you try and move to your side, and that doesn't work. After a while though, during the day, the crutches are a skoosh, and you become speedy and proficient, and popular because everyone wants to write their name on your leg with a touching little message. Your leg becomes a wall or a bus stop, graffiti. You are a walking work of art.

When the plaster comes off the leg still hasn't healed and the doctors are worried that they should have put a bit of metal in the leg rather than just let the bone meld together. There's a bend in the leg. They discuss re-breaking it then decide against it. They put my leg into a plastic splint and give me a walking stick. I'm seventeen with a brown walking stick. I ask them if I can paint it psychedelic colours, and they say, 'No, this walking stick belongs to the NHS and will have to be returned.' I feel self-conscious with my brown stick, getting on and off buses is a nightmare, getting up stairs into certain buildings is very tricky. I suddenly notice how much the whole architectural world is geared for the able-bodied. I notice how differently people treat me; it's as if they think I'm stupid just because I have a walking stick. They speak slower, louder, as if I'm deaf too.

I spend long slow hours on my own. I throw myself into reading. I read *Madame Bovary* and *Anna Karenina* and *10 Rillington Place* and *The Raj Quartet.* I re-read *Cider with Rosie* that we're studying at school, and *To Kill A Mockingbird*, and *The Catcher in the Rye.* Books are my friends. Holden Caulfield is misunderstood. I re-read *Wuthering Heights*. Heathcliff is adopted. *Wuthering Heights* is an adoption story gone badly wrong. Heathcliff is the dark force the kind family invited home; Heathcliff brings the whole house toppling down. *Jane Eyre* is also an adoption story. Jane is adopted by people that don't understand her fierce intelligence and put her in the red room, and then she's sort of semi-adopted by Mr Rochester who does understand her fierce intelligence and gives her the whole house. But the house still burns down. I read and read and look for meanings.

When I look back on that April of the compound fracture, I realize it is that, the broken leg and the long period of convalescence, which made me write. I suddenly saw the world differently and I knew that I wanted to write about what I saw. I wrote long poems about the accident, and apartheid and poverty and peace and housewives and anything else that interested me. When I went back to school after the long summer I showed my poems to my English teacher, Mrs Hughes, who showed them to her husband who showed them to Alasdair Gray, the writer and artist. I went to see him in his flat in Kersland Street in the west end of Glasgow. It was full of oil paints and pastels, brushes, and pencils, drawings and paintings. It was wild. I loved it. It looked like the flat of a real artist. He had trouble finding a clean cup to give me a cup of tea.

What I liked best were the words he said as he opened the door: 'Well, there's no doubt about it at all in my mind, in my mind, you are a writer.' Later, he looked over a three-page-long poem about the motorbike accident and put his pencil through most of it, saying, 'I think this poem would read better if you just put, "Suddenly stopped." ' But it didn't matter, I repeated those magic words on the way home, back through Ruchhill and Springburn to Bishopbriggs, 'I am a writer.' It seemed an outrageous and cheeky and grown-up statement, but I loved the sounds of the words long before I ever believed them. They seemed to grant me a lease of life, like somebody had suddenly given me an extra room to live in, a room that was all mine. Accidents, if you don't go and bloody die, can offer up a new way to live. Instead of doing hill starts and burpees, ham stretches and thigh stretches, and running fast round the red gravel running track, I had a new life of stationery, notebooks and pens. I had a new way of listening, but also, sadly, a different metabolism. I clearly needed all that exercise to stay slim. I put weight on and my body changed shape. I transformed from a slim but athletic-looking runner to a fat writer practically overnight. Now, this distance away from that accident, I can't imagine my life without it. It was the sudden fork in the road; the road I decided impulsively to take that did it.

19th March, 2009. Another spring evening, early pinkish light, shepherd's delight. I'm sitting round the dining-room table in the extension again, and my mum and dad are telling me stories about their days in New Zealand. A bottle of Chianti is open, and my dad's enjoying himself. They've been through a rough old time with my mum back and forth to hospital and kept in overnight twice on different occasions for nosebleeds that have lasted up to eight hours. My mum's collapsed from lack of blood and been given a blood transfusion for the first time in her life. One night in the hospital, when she was very weak and drained, a nurse said to her, 'Mrs Kay, I've an awkward question to ask – if you die in here would you like to see a minister?' My mum answered, quick as a flash, 'Only if he'll resuscitate me.'

Tonight my dad's equilibrium has returned because I'm here, and just as I used to only feel safe at night when my parents were back in the house, home from visiting Rita Baxter in Drymen or Nan and Jimmy Wilson in Kirkintilloch, or Pat Milligan in Drumchapel, or Charlie and Isabel Aird across the road, or Millie or Willie Moir in the Milton, so it seems that my parents now feel safer when they are with me. As if they have put some of their trust in me, and I'll sort things for them. My mum goes up to bed at her usual time, 10.30, and my dad and me stay down, finishing the wine, talk, talking. My dad even lights a wee cigar, relaxing at last.

At about midnight, there's an almighty crash and my mum has tripped over my dog at the bottom of the stairs and careened into the wall. Her head is cut, but not only that another nosebleed has started and been going on since she went to bed. 'But why didn't you call for us?' I say unable to cope with how it could have all been different, how she might just now have a nosebleed and not also a split head and a badly twisted ankle.

'I didn't want to bother you.'

'We'd better call for an ambulance,' I say, freaked out at the amount of blood that's pouring from her nose. I call Nick, who consults his doctor boyfriend Edward who says put ice on it. I call Denise, she says pinch the bridge of her nose and hold it for ten seconds. I try and talk in a soothing voice, but I'm terrified. My mum, who can moan about wee things, is stoical in crisis. She rises up and into herself, not a single complaint. I'm impressed with her bravery; it moves me almost to tears. 'Does your head hurt?' I say, frightened to look at the blood matted to her hair.

'Not really.' My dog skulks in the corner, guilty. 'Don't you feel guilty, Dinky,' my mum says to my dog, making the plump tears fall down my face. My dad keeps calm, but the evening has taken one of those turns that shock and distort the present. My mum fell over my dog and suddenly we're in another world, a kind of hell. I can't stop thinking if only my dog hadn't been lying at the bottom of the stairs, if only my mum had shouted for help. If only I'd gone up to check that she was OK after she went to bed. Accidents, small and large, spawn a whole series of *if onlys*. They come in shocked sputters, one after the other. There's always something you could have done differently. My mum sits quite calmly holding on to the bloodied kitchen roll. I run back and forth getting more. The blood runs down her pale pink nightdress and splatters on her wee pale slippers. It's like a horror movie. 'We have to call for an ambulance,' I repeat, and my dad finally agrees. He wanted to avoid my mum going to hospital again. He wanted to wait as long as possible and see if the nosebleed would stop. My mum doesn't want to go to hospital either but she's resigned herself. She suddenly looks smaller and older. The paramedics arrive at half-past one in the morning. 'I'm going with her, you go to bed,' I tell my dad.

My mum can't walk into the ambulance because her foot is so swollen. 'Not a part of me works,' she tries to joke. 'I need the scrap yard.' How noble the jokes are when the chips are down.

They strap her into a wheelchair and push her to the ambulance. The paramedics make me wait whilst they check her blood pressure and heartbeat in the ambulance. I know it's crazy but I light a cigarette and wait out in the street that I grew up in, still smoking, even at this late hour, the sky full of stars, a guilty, calming cigarette. Suddenly the ambulance door swings open and I toss the fag end away, but not quickly enough. 'Naughty!' says the paramedic; and I feel ashamed. I sit in the ambulance and hold my mum's hand. 'It's all right, you're going to be all right.' They've tied a contraption round her face, a kind of mask cum bandage, but the blood is still seeping through, relentless.

When we get to the Accident and Emergency of

Glasgow Royal Infirmary, the paramedics tell me to go one way and take my mum another. I'm suddenly stranded in a waiting room without her. I go up to the reception and ask them to let me be with her, which they do. If I hadn't done that she'd have been waiting through there on her own for three hours. I find my mum in one of the cubicles and hold her hand. She's focusing on being brave, and not talking much. The blood is still pouring and none of the staff are doing anything. They are standing around chatting to each other in the open booth in the middle of the ward. I keep going to them and asking for more bandages. She's getting through unbelievable amounts of bandages and tissues. The hospital is like some kind of war zone; nobody seems to be helping. I keep trying to do the pinch nose thing, but nothing's working. Eventually after forty-five minutes a young doctor appears, dark hair, tall, brisk. He says, 'Right, Mrs Kay, this is going to hurt and it might not work, I'm going to burn the inside of your nose.' And then he asks me to assist him. I shine a torch up my mum's nose, and he inserts implements. It's all brutal. He talks softly and she can't hear a word he's saying. He's slick and full of himself; has the horrible arrogance of the young doctor. He's treating her like she's stupid because she can't hear. I want to kill him.

'What age are you, Doctor?' I ask him.

'Thirty-two – why?' he says.

'Just because you seem really young,' I say. Then I say, 'This is Helen, I'm Jackie, what's your name?' to see if that will make any difference. I want to say, 'This is my mum, she used to be a primary teacher, she's very artistic, good company, still loves my dad, very on the ball, perceptive.' The doctor doesn't seem to be seeing a human being. He sees her age and translates her into a second-class citizen. I'm filled with a terrible rage and my mum is all vulnerable on the trolley of the waiting cubicle.

Everything the doctor says in his soft voice, I translate. 'What's he saying?' she says.

Finally the doctor thinks he might have been successful in cauterizing the other nostril. He looks at the wound at the back of the head, and puts some gel on it. He doesn't think it will need stitches, but tells my mum not to wash her hair until the wound heals. 'Can I go home?' my mum says. Her biggest fear has been that she'd be kept in.

'Yes,' the doctor says. 'You can go home.'

'Oh joy,' my mum says.

The staff nurse appears and says, 'If you want an ambulance to take her home, you'll have to wait hours. Do you want to book a taxi?'

'Yes,' I say, thinking the taxi driver and I will have to support her as she hobbles to her door. Another hospital orderly appears to tell me a taxi is here for me. She looks at me and then she looks at my mum and says, 'Are you taking the old biddy back to her care home?' My mum doesn't hear her, thank God.

'No, this is my mum,' I say. 'I'm taking her home.' All I can think of is that she's called my mum an old biddy, as if she never marched against apartheid, as if she was never gaoled for fighting Polaris, as if she'd never travelled through Russia on a train, as if she'd never met her love in New Zealand, as if she'd never adopted my brother, or me, as if she never nothing. Old biddy. Care home. I want to shake the orderly, to make her disorderly. A while later, I'm telling my French friend Catherine Marcangeli about this and she says, 'No, but this is racist too? She thought you were the care worker? No? She couldn't imagine you were her daughter?'

The taxi driver helps me help my mum to her front door at five in the morning. Doesn't matter the hour or that the birds are twittering or that the ankle's swollen and the head throbbing, the blood has stopped and she is home. My dad comes rushing down the stairs, surprised we've got her back. Between us we help my mum up the stairs, step by patient painful step.

Ages later, I tell her about the old biddy remark. 'Is that what she said?' she says. 'Bloody cheek!'

'I know, what a nerve!' I say and we both laugh. From the safe distance of the head healed and the ankle down, and the nose freed from the horrendous nosebleeds, the *old biddy* story strikes us as hilarious. My mum is a modern woman, trendy in her necklaces and trousers and tops. She always looks fabulous, never even touched a twin set, or a pleated skirt. *Old biddy!* I tell her of Catherine's interpretation. 'That's probably true,' she says; 'saw you as a care-home worker! What a scream. You'd make an excellent care-home orderly!'

2009

Last night I dreamt I was on the red-dust road again. I was walking bare foot. The elephant grasses were greener than ever in my dream, and gigantic, reaching for the bright blue sky. I walked along the road round the first bend and then the second. When I looked behind me, I saw the birds. They flew down to land on the banana tree next to me, the babblers, the bustards, the white-eyes, the helmet shrikes, the hoopoes, the turacos, the wattle-eyes, the old-world flycatchers, the nightjars. I stopped walking and they flew down and some of them rested on my head, and others on my shoulders. They were singing together like a choir sings; each wattle-eye letting the babbler's chirp come through. I started to dance on the road; my feet found a dance I didn't know I knew, and the birds danced with me, swooping in the air, whirling, and spinning, making letters of the alphabet and then composing numbers in the sky, figures of eight. The sweat poured down my face and into the red earth. I danced on. A goat appeared on the road and danced with me. The goat's beard was very distinguished-looking. I couldn't believe how green the green was and how red the red. Away in the distance, a gun went off. The road split in two, and I couldn't decide which way to go. I wondered if I could get lost, if I might just get lost in the bush. I took the left-hand fork. I danced further down the red-dust road, and turned another bend and another. I danced into the sound of the drums beating, softly, at first, fragile, like the beat of a babbler's heart. Then the drums got louder and I saw my brother's face. Only in my dream he was a baby. He was a beautiful dark baby. He came toddling towards me with his arms outstretched on the road. I picked him up and held him in my arms. In my dream, I walked with my baby brother all the way into the village.

Enugu back to Lagos

September 30th, 2009

Today is Wednesday and we're off to Enugu. I decide that I want to take some of the *kai kai* back home, so Pious drives back to the market, and Kachi rushes out and buys us a bottle apiece, liquor that Bessie Smith would have loved, rough moonshine. I imagine her raunchy voice singing, '*Gimme a pigfoot and a bottle of gin.*' But today the market is totally deserted. The wooden stalls look sad and unpeopled as if the bustle and excitement of the market yesterday was just a dream somebody had. Kachi finds somewhere that sells the special fried breadfruit seeds in a bottle, *ukwa*, that his mother-in-law has asked him to get. They are particularly good in this part of Anambra, he says.

Another extraordinary coincidence: when Kachi rang Uncle Nwora to say he was going to be in Enugu, Uncle Nwora told Kachi that on Wednesday he had a botanical meeting with the Professor O that Kachi had previously been asking about. Very bizarre timing, timing which could lead me to think that if God is on anyone's side it is mine. Now Kachi phones Nwora and asks if he is still meeting Professor O and he says *Yes*. Between four and six. It is 3.25 on my watch. I can't get over the fact that Kachi's uncle Nwora is meeting my father just as we are driving towards Enugu. I've become so accustomed to reading everything in signs. I have done this all my life; but now that I'm in Nigeria, my obsession with what things mean suddenly seems to make sense, because everybody does it. It is an Igbo way. 'What does this mean?' I ask Kachi excitedly. 'It must mean something!' I ask Kachi to call him on the cell number that Jonathan's cousin gave us.

'Really?' says Kachi. 'You're sure?'

'Yes. Don't say that you know I am his daughter, just say that you are on a research trip with Professor Kay, and that we'd like half an hour of his time. He probably doesn't know I'm here. The email address must have been out of date.'

So Kachi calls and he gets through. I'm sitting next to Kachi in the back of the car. Pious seems to be listening intently whilst driving the car, holding his head very still in listening position at the steering wheel. He's turned down the radio. Kachi says, 'Hello, is this Professor O?' My father, on the other side of the line, obviously confirms. Kachi says, 'Good afternoon, Professor, my name is Kachi. I'm with Professor Jackie Kay. We are coming towards Enugu and she wondered if she might meet with you.' Kachi looks awkward and surprised. He says, 'Well, we are here for a few days, do you have any time

246

you could spare? She wouldn't need to take up too much of your time.'

Kachi listens and looks embarrassed. 'All right then, sir, good afternoon.' Kachi turns to me and reports back on the half of the conversation I couldn't hear. 'I told him you were here and he said he was busy. I then asked when he might have time for us and he said he couldn't see himself having any time – that he got your email.'

'He got my email?' I say incredulously.

'Yes, he got your email.' Kachi looks down, as if not looking directly at me might spare my shame. 'Then, he said,' Kachi continues, '"Tell her I wish her well and that she should go ahead from here." I think he said go ahead, he might have said move on from here. It was something like that, Jackie,' Kachi says very awkwardly in his low, quiet voice. I shake my head; my face floods with tears. Kachi says, 'I'll leave you alone for a bit, Jackie,' and gets out of the car. He is clearly upset himself. Pious sits silent at the wheel listening. He says nothing. Kachi returns to the car.

'I can't believe he got my email and he never replied,' I say. 'There were so many different replies he could have given. If he'd just said then, "No, I can't see you again, but I wish you well," that would have been better than this.'

Kachi says, 'Jackie, he doesn't deserve you. Forget it. Forget him. It makes me so angry.'

Pious says, 'Sir, what kind of man is this? It pains me that you wouldn't want to see your own blood!' He hisses and shakes his head. We drive off through the inventive police roadblocks of broken branches of trees and old tyres, old stationary wheels not going round and round.

That night we arrive at a hotel called Toscana in Independence Lay Out, Enugu. Pious and Kachi admire the good roads in Enugu, the working street lights, the clean streets and the hard-working governor. We go and visit Kachi's in-laws. I'm looking forward to meeting his mother-in-law in particular since she is also from Ukpor. His father-in-law, a tall and shimmering man, elegantly dressed in a long black dress and black trousers, welcomes me with the traditional Igbo welcome of kola nuts and the elaborate blessing. The man performs it beautifully. He's a character; he mixes well grace with flamboyance.

'Take the nut away home and it will open its mouth and talk to you and yours at home. I am humbled to be with a distinguished guest who is here recording values that transcend space and time,' he says. 'When you get home Oji speaks. It tells where it has come from. Oji, the kola nut, is the symbol of sincere welcome, truth, sincerity, good-will, peace and joy, happiness and prayer,' he says. 'Pray to the ancestors and the Most High for protection, progress, long life, guidance and fertility! When obstacles and sad shadows obscure the light on our path,' he says, 'we must not lose heart. After every cloudy sky comes glorious sunshine!' His voice rises and falls theatrically. 'The Most High, Almighty wills only goodness, love and justice for us all. Jackie is a true daughter of Ukpor. Amen.'

Kachi's mother-in-law, a small woman, much lighter-skinned than her husband, with a similar-shaped face to my own, has cooked a veritable feast – steamed fish, roast chicken thighs and legs, jollof rice, plantains, vegetable curry, green salad with cucumber. It's all absolutely delicious. I wash down the meal with a gourd of palm wine. I tell them about Jonathan not wanting to meet me and find myself weeping again at the dinner table. Kachi's mother-in-law is furious. 'He is treating you like a *bastard* and you are not a *bastard*. I wish I had known, I would have taken you to Ukpor myself and introduced you to everyone as his daughter. You shouldn't collude with him. Why should you agree to keep yourself a secret! It's wrong.'

Her elegant husband interrupts her. 'Look,' he says, gently touching my arm, 'we need to think of a different way to deal with this. I could call your father and tell him to come to my office and say, "Sir, good day, what are the five precepts of life that are most important to you." He would come, of course he would come, because I am a commissioner. I would sit him down and calmly say—'

'Calmly?' his wife interrupts furiously, talking in a strong Igbo accent. 'I know how to deal with this. I'm from the same place. I'm from Ukpor.' She turns to me. 'You are my sister. When you are from the same place, it means you are automatically my sister. Look at us. We even look like sisters.'

'In order to understand something complex you have to be able to see it from the other person's point of view,' the elegant father-in-law says. 'What do you think his point of view is, Jackie?'

I am just about to answer when Kachi pipes up. 'Daddy,' Kachi interrupts. 'This has been all very upsetting for Jackie. This is serious,' he says, thinking that his father-in-law is enjoying the dilemma too much.

'Let me finish,' his father-in-law says, determinedly. 'Now, we need to deal with this situation above the way the crowd would deal with it,' he says in his slow impeccable posh English accent. 'We are not riff-raff.'

'Riff-raff?' his mother-in-law says.

'Listen!' he says, holding both of his long hands together as if in prayer. 'We are special. Now, Jackie, listen. I would ask him, "What are the five precepts by which you govern your life?" I would invite him here. I would sit him down first. "Sit down, sir!" I would say. He would come; of course he would come because I am a commissioner. I promise you, Jackie, I would listen, I would discuss and by the time I had finished with him, talking in this decent way, the man would have tears of redemption pouring down his cheeks. I am telling you, your father would be crying tears of redemption.'

Kachi shakes his head. He can't believe that his father-in-law has gone in for the amateur dramatics. I'm feeling quite entertained, and touched that they feel involved and have such strong opinions but the vision of my father being frogmarched into an office and questioned is of no comfort to me.

'I wouldn't like that,' I say. 'He is my father.'

Kachi says, 'Daddy, you cannot force somebody to feel

something they don't feel. A cornered man is a dangerous man.'

'What danger can he do me?' his father-in-law says. 'The man would be begging for forgiveness. I still think we could find a way to reach him. It is he who would cry once I had talked in this sophisticated way.'

Kachi's mother-in-law starts off again, 'Who needs this sophistication? Listen to me, Jackie. These are *my* people! My husband is not from the same part of Nigeria, so he knows *nothing*. I am proud of you, even if your father isn't. I will take you there and you will get the welcome you deserve.' It is just not done here. It is so unusual for a man not to acknowledge his blood; at least, I think to myself, it is some consolation that, by Nigerian standards, my father is a highly unusual man.

That night we leave Kachi's in-laws, their seven dogs bark under the pitch-black starless sky, rushing up to us as we get into the back of the car. Enugu feels a safe city even in the dark, the flat roads well lit. 'I'd like to spend longer here some time,' I say to Kachi, who is still shaken by the conversation with Jonathan.

He says, 'Forget him now, Jackie. I can't believe it. He doesn't deserve you,' as if I've said something about my father. Kachi and I sit outside in the hotel's gardens and have one last beer. The clock strikes midnight. It is now Independence Day. I toast Kachi and his new book *The Shadow of A Smile* and he toasts me, smiling shyly. 'To Independence,' we both say, clinking our glasses to all the meanings *independence* now has for us. I feel quite happy and strangely liberated. So my father doesn't want to see me? So that is that. I can now do what I want. I can even contact my brother if I want. 'Perhaps my father has done me a favour? Yes,' I say to Kachi, two palm wines, one red wine and one bottle of a beer from the Nigerian Breweries down me, 'time to . . . what did he say? Move ahead? Go ahead?'

'Something like that,' Kachi says.

'OK, then! Time to move ahead,' I say in my version of a Nigerian accent that my friends tell me is not bad, not bad at all: *move ahead. Move ahead from here. Go ahead. Go ahead from here.*

Kachi giggles at my accent and we toast again. 'To Independence!' we say, significantly. The starless dark night sky is our placid, loyal witness.

October 1st, 2009

Today – it is forty-nine years since the end of British rule in Nigeria. I decide to go for a swim in the pool in the Toscana Hotel. Pious is outside already standing by the car. 'Good morning, madam,' he says. I tell him I'm going towards the pool and he can join me if he likes. But the pool is emptied of water. They are filling it with chemicals and it won't be ready to swim in till this evening. Pious and I order some juice, pineapple and coconut for him, and orange and pineapple for me, and two donuts and sit at a table in the hotel garden. A young woman, whose skin is a kind of purple black, a glowing aubergine colour, brings our food over, and says to me, 'Happy Independence Day, madam.'

Pious sucks in his breath in irritation. 'I have no time for Happy Independence Day,' he says. 'Not when the roads are full of potholes, when the children have to go to Ghana or England or South Africa to get an education, when there's so much corruption, when a country who has all this oil can't sort out its electricity. When we have power cuts every day! When the rich are very rich and the poor are very poor. No, madam. It is not Happy Independence Day for me!' He sucks his lips again. 'Happy Independence Day! I've no time for it. This country could do so much better.' He pronounces better as *betta*. *This country could do so much betta.*

I go to my room to pack up. Soon we'll be going to visit Kachi's Uncle Sunday and then on to Enugu airport to fly back to Lagos. We arrive at Uncle Sunday's house. A man pulls open the gates and we go into his courtyard. Lizards dart about. We get led into the hall and sit and wait a while. Nwora drops by. Kachi, excited and happy, greets him, 'The *professorial elephant!*'

'Kedu?' I say to Nwora and he laughs at my pronunciation, and says something back that I don't understand.

'Nsogbu adiro. Ginwa kwanu? If you can say Kedu you must learn Ginwa kwanu.'

'So you are Professor *Moringa Oleifera*?' I say, and Kachi says, 'What a memory you have, Jackie!'

And I say, 'Well, of course,' because *Moringa oleifera* is the plant that connects his family to mine, and the reason that we found Jonathan's phone number and the names of two of my brothers. I even like the way the name sounds, since it has brought its own peculiar magic to my story, and it is a magic tree. Nwora looks delighted.

'Actually,' he says, 'moringa grows here.'

I follow him outside to the courtyard full of trees and plants and he cuts some branches of the moringa tree. 'Smell,' he says. It has a spicy distinctive smell, healing. Later Nwora tells us all about *Moringa oleifera*: how the leaves are used to treat malnutrition, how they can have a stabilizing effect on blood pressure, and treat anxiety; how the leaf juice can be used as a diuretic and the leaf sap as a purgative, and the leaves can be used to treat malaria and jaundice. The leaves, the roots, the pods and the flowers, the root bark and stem bark all have multiple medicinal purposes. He returns to his house to collect moringa pods for me, and comes back, sweating, half an hour later with a small black plastic bag. 'You soak these for half an hour then dry them with tissue paper, then plant them directly into the soil. Soon you will have your own moringa growing. It is hardy.' His three-year-old daughter, dressed in a pretty white lacy dress, stands in front of me and confidently recites the names of the different moringas like a litany: '*Moringa oleifera, Moringa peregrina, Moringa stenopetala.*' It must be all mysterious to her, the work of her tree-specialist father, and she, tiny though she is, knows instinctively that the route to her father's heart is through his plants and roots.

Uncle Nwora's face shines with pride. 'You see? You see how she can pronounce the names?'

I imagine that if the other road had been taken, I might have learnt off by heart names of moringa trees to please my father.

Uncle Sunday comes into the room, a small, round, affable-looking man. He is still wearing his pyjamas. He shakes my hand warmly. 'My name is Godson Sunday,' he tells me. 'My father was an evangelist. I've been a father to many children, some of them my own, some not. What fascinates me is what makes a child, who they are because each of my children here has had the same opportunities, and yet some have done well and some have not. How to explain it? Is it in the genes? Is it the way they are brought up? Or do I call it God? Do I call it God's will?'

'This question fascinates me,' I say, leaning forward in my chair to be closer to him. 'Nature or nurture?'

'Exactly!' Uncle Sunday says. 'Nature or nurture or God.' He holds Kachi's book in his hand and examines it. He's obviously delighted and proud. Uncle Sunday studied at Strathclyde University in Glasgow. 'I have so many fond memories of Glasgow,' he says. 'How is the dear old place?'

When I get Kachi on his own for a few minutes, I say to him, 'I think you should tell Nwora that Jonathan is my father.' (I had asked Kachi at the beginning to keep it secret.) 'It's crazy. One person being secretive throws others into uncomfortable situations.' Kachi agrees.

I go out to the car to talk to Pious and when I come back, Kachi whispers, 'I've told them.'

Uncle Nwora looks at me and whistles! 'Now that I know, I can see it clearly. You have his forehead, same height, build, shape of face,' he laughs, excited. 'It is all there! Goodness, goodness, goodness!'

'I wish I'd known yesterday, when Nwora was meeting him,' Uncle Sunday says to Nwora. 'I would have taken you with me and confronted him. It's madness not to acknowledge your blood.'

'It's his religion,' I say.

'That's not religion,' Uncle Sunday says.

'No one dare ask him these days to do the blessing. He just goes on and on, dancing, singing, praying. He never used to be like that,' Nwora says, laughing.

'Perhaps it is since his first wife died?' I say.

'Yes . . . I think you are right. He took it hard.'

'Perhaps his religion houses grief, deafens grief, or perhaps grief makes you kind of deaf to everything else, and the only listening ear is God's?' I say. I feel a little like I have to defend my father's behaviour.

'I still don't call that religion,' Uncle Sunday says.

Uncle Sunday's niece brings us hot pepper fish soup to eat still sitting in the living room on the sofa. We each have a small tray. She brings a bottle of wine. Uncle Sunday apologizes. It was meant to be white wine, he says, and then red for the main course.

'Not to worry, it's lovely,' I say, greatly cheered to be having wine at lunchtime.

'You know I used to go to school with Jonathan O,' Uncle Sunday says.

'Really?' I say, the coincidences piling up like a stack of wobbly books.

'Yes, he was in the senior year, when I was a few years down.'

'What was he like?' I'm still despite myself, and despite the recent phone call, fascinated to hear about Jonathan as a boy.

'He was very bright. One year when we didn't have a science teacher, he continued to teach himself. He got hold of books and used to memorize scientific charts. Yes, he was very bright, always interested in how things worked. You could tell he would go far.'

Nwora adds; 'The man is renowned around the world for his work on trees and plants. Even he has lost count of the amount of papers he has published. I mean, he's internationally known. This is what makes all this fanaticism so sad. He's a clever man. You would think that he would be able to see that this was in his past, that he's done nothing wrong, that there's no need for such a secret to be kept. You are a grown woman. You've grown like a plant away from him, but it is still his roots. You have his face. You have his forehead!' Nwora laughs. He's still amazed. He turns to Kachi and says, 'So this is why you've been asking all the time about O? I wondered. I thought, Why is Kachi so interested in the Professor? Well, now I know!'

257

'I think he worries about how he would be seen,' I say. 'He worries that the knowledge of me would undermine his Church. He told me the only way he could possibly acknowledge me would be if I agreed to be born again, and then he could say, this woman is my past, my sin. This is my future.'

Both Nwora and Uncle Sunday shake their heads in disbelief. 'It is not the Igbo way,' they say sadly.

'Just yesterday the Professor was praying for me,' Nwora said. 'If I'd known this then, I'd have prayed for *him*!'

'Let's go through to lunch,' Uncle Sunday says. We move from the lovely living room with wooden staircase into a large dining room. We sit down at a splendid table laden with food, a feast: chicken legs, rice, plantain, fish heads, salad, a beautiful bright orange pumpkin stew, and big black snails. Uncle Sunday points out the snails, which are a delicacy. 'You must try one,' he says. And I do. I'm a bit squeamish though about crunching through the snail, and it's very tough. 'It's all good white meat,' Uncle Sunday says seeing my hesitation and pouring me a glass of wine, 'It's a Bordeaux,' he says proudly.

'Lovely wine,' I say, a little later.

'It's a Bordeaux,' Uncle Sunday says again, pleased with the fine French wine ending up in his dining room in Enugu, Nigeria. Everything travels these days, I think, swigging my wine.

Small Uncle Sunday and tall Uncle Nwora stand in the porch waving us goodbye, two brothers of very different

258

heights, but equal kindness. 'They are lovely, your uncles,' I say to Kachi.

'I know!' Kachi says and laughs, a little high laugh.

'They are obviously very proud of you,' I say and Kachi beams, his handsome face lit up by his smile.

Pious drives Kachi and me to Enugu airport and we get on the plane back to Lagos, an hour's journey compared to the thirteen-hour journey by car. I'm glad though that we did the journey that way, it felt like an odyssey, and happy too that we opted for returning by plane. I hug Pious good-bye. I feel like we've been through such a lot together, and that I've got to know him quite well. 'Take care, driving back, Pious, and *thank you*, thank you so much. I hope we see each other again.' Pious nods proudly and hugs me back. 'You too. Look after yourself. Don't worry any more about *that* father.'

It's amazing to be back in the buzz, the hustle and bustle of Lagos, where cars seem to invent new spaces to drive through and the idea of traffic lanes seems anachronistic. Back in the beeping, tooting, scorching, brightly coloured, musical Lagos, I feel like a returner, from the east to the city. The traffic seems completely normal to me now, and the buzz and fizz of the city wel-comingly exciting. *I love Lagos*. I loved the east too, but it's good to be back in the relative anonymity of the city. I like the energy of the place. Here nobody will shout *Oyibo*, or pause for two seconds over the colour of my skin. It's good to be back and to recognize things: Eko Bridge, Lagos Harbour, Awolowo Road, Ikoyi, which reminds me

259

that the bookstore I haven't yet visited, Jazz Hole, is on this road. Now it feels great to know when I'm in Victoria Island and when I'm in Lagos Island, when I'm going round the busy bustling King George roundabout, and not to feel fazed by going round it any more. For all the crazy driving in Lagos, I've yet to see an accident, which means that Nigerian drivers are either the world's worst or actually the world's best. There's such ingenuity involved in negotiating a roundabout in Lagos.

Later, I tell Chimamanda about my trip to Ukpor and about Kachi talking to Jonathan as we were heading for Enugu. Chimamanda is so surprised that Jonathan had received my email after all. 'He got the email?' Her eyes narrow, protectively, eyebrow archly raised. 'He got the email?'

A text comes through from Denise saying she really thinks I should contact Sidney now and that it is my right. Five minutes later a text arrives from Kachi saying exactly the same thing.

Chimamanda says, 'Well, how do you feel about that?'

'I'm not sure,' I say, feeling a bit flat and defeated.

'I'm worried about the emotional cost,' Chimamanda says. 'What if Sidney turns out to be a younger version of his father?'

'Yes,' I say. 'I'm in two minds. I want Sidney to know that I exist but I'm not up to another rejection.'

'Let's sleep on it,' Chimamanda says, wisely. Then she says, surprising me, 'You seem to be feeling guilty. You are not doing anything wrong.'

I don't know how she knows to say this to me, she seems to have a quite uncanny ability to see right through me, it's true, and I am feeling guilty. It has been the burning question for me for years: do I have the right to suddenly expose my father's secret to his son? Is it right for me to turn up and announce myself when he has been hell-bent on keeping me hidden? What damage might I cause to his family? Am I being selfish in wanting to meet my siblings when he clearly wants nothing more to do with me? *And so on. And so forth.* I've set the firework off inside the house and who knows whether it can easily be put out, or if it will rage through the house till the whole place burns down. 'You're right,' I say to Chimamanda. 'I am feeling a bit guilty. I don't know what is right.'

'You have the right,' she says.

'Why do you give your father all this consideration?' Chioma, Chimamanda's friend, says. 'Has he given that to you? Has he thought about *you* the way you are thinking about him? Don't cry any more tears for that man, he doesn't deserve them. What is this loyalty? What is it?'

I try and silently answer Chioma's question, picking up another chicken leg and nibbling on it. I'm not sure where the loyalty comes from, and even though I'm hurt I still don't want anything bad to happen to Jonathan. He must feel that what he did to my mother in the past, getting her pregnant outside of wedlock, was a sin so terrible that it cannot be brought back into his present. At least, even if erroneously, he is taking the business of getting a young woman pregnant seriously. Perhaps the responsibility for it has ruptured him in some way. But then I remember asking him in Abuja if he had ever thought about me, and I also remember his reply: 'No, never, why would I have done that?'

October 2nd, 2009

Chimamanda, ill and peaky with malaria, sits wearily at the breakfast table. Kola brings us three perfect tomato-and-red-pepper omelettes, the tomatoes and peppers diced into tiny pieces. Chimamanda, though ill, asks *me* how I am and looks carefully to assess whether or not I'm telling her the truth when I reply, 'Fine.' She asks me if I've had any more thoughts about contacting Sidney. 'I think I should. It feels like now or never. I just need to be bold enough. Kachi sent another text; he has found Sidney's cell number.'

'OK,' Chimamanda says, 'let us plot what to say.'

'You could say that you are with a friend who wants to see him about a personal matter,' I say.

'Won't he ask what?' she says.

'Yes, so just say she'd prefer not to discuss it over the phone and she would like to meet you.'

'Should I say it concerns his father?' Chimamanda asks.

'No, he might worry,' I say. 'Let's just try that and see what he says.'

'Wait, I'm trying to think what I would do if somebody called me saying that. I might think it was a crank call.'

'I know, but you might be curious . . . Anyway, I don't want to make up a lie and then have to tell him that that was a lie, so this is our only option.'

Chimamanda takes a couple of deep breaths to psych herself up to make the call. 'Hello, my name is Chimamanda Adichie,' she says, politely, 'I have a friend here, Jackie Kay, from England who would like to meet you to discuss a personal matter.' I can't hear the other side of the call but from Chimamanda's expressions it is not going well. I'm starting to feel the whole thing is crazy, and that this is a big mistake. I actually feel frightened and guilty as if I'm doing something terribly wrong. Chimamanda keeps talking in a calm, reasoned voice, though I can tell it's costing her. She gets off the phone and shakes her head sadly. 'He won't meet unless he knows what it's about. It's fair enough, really. Why would you want to arrange to meet a complete stranger if you haven't been told the reason?

'Let's take the advice of the elders,' Chimamanda says, only in this case it is the advice of the *youngers*. She calls Chioma, who thinks that Sidney might already know. She rings Kachi. Kachi thinks we have no alternative but to tell him on the phone. 'They are both adults. One hundred per cent,' Kachi says.

Chimamanda tries ringing Sidney again but his phone rings out. 'He's not picking up,' she says. 'Maybe he's having a bad day. I'll text him,' she says. She sends a text which says: *Sorry to be in touch out of the blue, my friend is returning to England tonight and would really like to meet you.*

Chimamanda goes off to lie down. She's exhausted. I worry that the drama of the blood is draining hers. I decide to take a swim; there's nothing like a swim when your head is swimming. It's the best cure. I swim breaststroke for twenty lengths. Being carried by the water is a big relief for my hugely swollen feet, swollen beyond all recognition by the heat. Then I lie on my back and float, not using my hands or legs to power me, just floating, just staying buoyant. I tilt my face to the African sun. Some sense of optimism is starting to float alongside me.

Okey and the swimming-pool attendant gasp in amazement at my floating. 'How do you do that?' Okey, who can't swim, says, shuddering almost as if it gives him the heebie-jeebies, as if I'm doing something freakish.

'I'm just floating, it's easy,' I say, feeling flattered and euphoric, like I'm performing some minor miracle.

'Yes, but you're not using your. arms or legs. It's strange,' Okey says and laughs. The swimming-pool attendant comes closer to. watch; he also marvels at my floating, making an admiring noise, *eh-eh.*

Chimamanda emerges at the side of the pool. She's had a reply to her text. Sidney has written back: *On what, please.*

'I will have to tell him over the phone then,' I say. We try Sidney's number, but again he's not answering his phone.

'Maybe he's in a meeting,' Chimamanda says. 'He sounded like he was having a busy day, sounded a bit harassed. Let's leave it for a few hours. I need to lie down.'

'Let's try again around five; he might be finished with his meetings by then.' I start to feel a bit anxious again. Perhaps I should leave it? Forget it? But I can't. I'm curious even to hear his voice on the phone. I decide to go out to Jazz Hole Bookshop to keep me occupied till five. At Jazz Hole, I relax a bit, search the shelves for an Igbo dictionary, for a book on Igbo customs and beliefs. I don't find either. I buy some music instead; *High Life Kings*, a compilation of Igbo music with performing artists Chief Stephen Oisita Osadebe, Professional Seagulls Dance Band, Sir Victor Uwaifo, Celestine Ukwu, Inyang Henshaw. I buy a big map of Nigeria in the sister bookshop along Awowolo Road and a tiny book on Igbo etymology, and another on Nigerian festivals by Pelu Awofeso, one of the writers that attended the Farafina Workshop. I'm starting to feel much better. I buy a paperback of Chimamanda's *The Thing Around My Neck* even though I have an English copy already. I like the idea of having a Nigerian one. I buy a big anthology called *Camouflage, Best of Contemporary Writing from Nigeria*. The whole lot costs a huge amount of naira; retail therapy doesn't come cheap.

It is four o'clock. I'm leaving Lagos at eleven tonight, and have to be at the airport by nine. Okey says we need to leave around seven for the airport because of

Friday-night Lagos traffic. If I am going to see Sidney today there is not much time left. The clock is ticking. I get back into the car and arrive at Chimamanda's just before five. Chimamanda is lying in her bed doing her emails on her laptop. I go upstairs to pack and sort my stuff and change. I change into my best turquoise shirt. It is now quarter past five. I suddenly decide that the time is right to call Sidney. This time I know I'll get through. 'If I'm going to call Sidney I need to call him right now,' I say to Chimamanda. She dials Sidney's number and hands the phone to me. 'Hello, is that Sidney?'

A voice at the other end of the line says hesitantly, 'Yes?' His voice is deep and rich. I take a deep breath.

'Sidney, my friend called earlier. My name is Jackie Kay. I can understand you being cautious about meeting me when you don't know what it is about. I hadn't wanted to tell you on the phone. Shall I just tell you then on the phone?'

He says, 'Yes.' I start to tell him and then become aware that nobody is on the end of the line. 'I think he hung up,' I say to a Chimamanda who is on tenterhooks. 'Or maybe we just got cut off. I don't know if he heard what I was saying.'

Sidney calls back. 'This is a good sign,' Chimamanda says, 'he's calling back!' She passes the phone to me. 'Remember, Jackie, talk slowly!'

'Hello? Sidney?' I feel like I'm going to explode with nerves. 'I don't know if you heard me or not?'

'I can hear you now,' Sidney says. 'Go ahead.'

'Well, my name is Jackie Kay. Your father is Jonathan O?'

'Yes?' Sidney says. I can almost hear him thinking, What is this about?

'He went to Aberdeen University?'

'Yes?'

'. . . Where he met my birth mother. Jonathan O is my birth father.'

There's a pause. 'Is my father *aware*?' Sidney asks.

'Yes, he's *aware*. I met him in 2003. He came to the Nicon Hotel in Abuja to meet me. I just came from Enugu and tried to see him again.'

There's another pause and then Sidney says, 'So you are my sister!' And he laughs a high laugh exactly like my own. 'Eh, eh, you are my sister!' he repeats.

'Yes, I am, yes, yes,' I say, 'I am your sister.'

'Where is your mother?' Sidney asks.

'I didn't grow up with my mother. I was adopted by two lovely people and brought up in Scotland.'

'Where are you now?' Sidney asks.

'I'm in Ikoyi,' I say. 'Wait, I'll hand the phone back to my friend to arrange things.'

Chimamanda takes the phone. 'New Nation Stadium?' she says. I'm feeling high. He said, *You are my sister.* He said, *You are my sister.*

Chimamanda jumps into action. 'Okey,' she says to her brother, 'you will have to go with Jackie and then on to the airport. The stadium is on the way to the airport. Jackie, you will have to hurry. Quick! You need to get going. You won't have much time. It is five thirty.' I rush up the stairs and throw the last couple of things in my suitcases. I feel all of a dither. I put some more lipstick on. 'That's a nice shirt!' Chimamanda says. 'You should have worn that for your reading. It is elegant.'

'Thank you,' I say. 'It cost me a fortune.'

Chimamanda smiles. I smile too: a sartorial compliment from Chimamanda Adichie is not to be taken lightly. 'Hurry! Hurry!' she says again.

I jump up and down on the spot and clap my hands. 'He sounded so nice. He sounded lovely!'

'Hurry, Jackie! You have so little time!' Chimamanda says, agitated.

It is by now a quarter to six and my flight leaves at eleven. I have to be at Lagos International Airport by nine at the latest. When I first came to Nigeria this time, I knew I would go and find my father's village; I never imagined that I would find and meet my brother. Okey opens the door of the black Range Rover. It's quite a high step up. I have to heave myself in and hurl myself into the seat. Next time I come to Nigeria, I promise to be in better shape, I say to myself. Okey introduces me to the driver, also called Sunday. 'How long will it take to reach the stadium?'

'It's not far,' Okey says, patiently. 'It's just the traffic.'

Friday-night Lagos traffic is not the traffic you want on the road on the way to meet your brother for the first time. We've been stuck in a jam for over an hour now. It seems that the world's cars have crowded in to cross this same Eko bridge. It's hard to imagine other cars anywhere else in the world, in Perth, in Cape Town, in London, in Glasgow, in San Francisco on bridges or at traffic lights. No, they all appear to have come to Lagos. 'I'd like a free and open road! I'd like the whole road to ourselves,' I say to a smiling Okey, who takes my hand and pats it. 'I'd like all the cars to disappear so that I can meet my brother.'

'We'll get there,' Okey says, laughing.

'But will he still be there by the time we get there?'

'He'll be there,' Okey says, patting my hand again. 'Calm down, Jackie,' he says and giggles helplessly. We both giggle; we've come full circle Okey and me. The trip began with us laughing our heads off when he picked me up at the airport, it seems many moons ago, when we laughed at how long the light stays in the summers in Finland, and how long it's possible to see your own shadow for, and how people cycle about at two in the morning in the bright light. We had tears pouring down our faces. And Pious was driving back then, though I didn't know him yet. It was twelve days ago, but it feels like much longer than that. I feel I've grown older in the space of the two journeys; the first car driven by Pious and the second by Sunday.

An hour and twenty minutes into our nudge by nudge, car by car journey, Chimamanda calls to say that Sidney rang her again, and apologized for seeming rude earlier, and thanked her for persevering and for helping me to find him. He's very sweet, Chimamanda says, sounding girlish and excited. 'Jackie, Sidney asked how long you've been here, and I said a week and a half and he groaned A WEEK AND A HALF! He asked if you can't stay a bit longer and get a flight back another time. I said, no you have to fly tonight. And then he asked what you want, if you want to come and live in Nigeria!' Chimamanda laughs, a trilling laugh, like she's happily ensconced inside a story.

'Really?' I say, touched.

'I told him. You have your own life. You don't want anything except to meet. Oh, Jackie, he sounds very excited. Just thought I'd fill you in before you get there. How near are you now?'

'How near are we, Okey?'

'Not far,' Okey says. 'Maybe not more than ten minutes now.'

I'm forty-seven. I imagine Sidney will be forty-five, forty-four. Ten minutes to go. It's taken us an hour and a half to get across Lagos. Ten minutes more. It's all down to timing. What's ten minutes out of my forty-seven years? They tick slowly; time is so subjective; time is such a tease. It is the same ten minutes that might slip by unnoticed any other day; but today it crawls, car by car, inch by inch, billboard by billboard, hawker by hawker, church sign by church sign. It is nearly seven fifteen. 'How long from the stadium to the airport?'

Okey shrugs. 'Need to allow an hour at least. The traffic to the airport will be terrible too.'

'So we won't have more than an hour together, will we?'

Suddenly, we turn right and are facing the entrance of the New Nation Stadium. Okey calls Sidney to say we are nearly there. Sidney asks what car we are in. Okey says, 'We're in a black Range Rover with some writing on its side.'

Sidney says, 'Come through the entrance and I'll be waiting.' We stop at the gates to pay the twenty-naira entrance fee. We drive on through, looking from side to side. I'm searching wildly for a man who looks like my brother. The stadium is busy. I almost can't see anything for looking too hard.

Suddenly Okey says, '*There he is! Stop!*' At the very same moment, Sidney spots us and runs alongside the Range Rover thumping on its sides to get the driver to stop. Sunday drives on a little and Sidney keeps running alongside until the Range Rover finally brakes, all in a matter of long-distance seconds. I open the door and jump down the steps. Sidney is standing there, a green cap on, wearing a green, white and yellow T-shirt, with his arms wide open. He takes me in his arms and holds me swaying me from side to side and saying, 'Eh, eh,' over and over again. He stops swaying me to stare into my face. There are tears in his eyes, and tears in mine. He hugs me tightly again and then takes my hand. We walk toward the outside stadium cafe together, hand in hand, comfortable, brother and sister, as if we'd known each other all of our lives.

Sidney is much taller than I expected, at least five ten or eleven. He leads Okey and me to a Chinese-style take-away within the stadium grounds. 'What do you want to drink?' he asks me, determined to get drinks in fast, and food, aware of the short time we have.

I hesitate, and then decide best to start the way I mean to continue, 'A beer, please.'

'And something to eat?' Sidney says. 'They have these chips.' He scans the menu quickly and calls the waitress over. 'What do you have that's quick? Are these quick?' He points to some deep-fried prawns. She nods. 'You're sure, they are quick?' She nods again. 'Three of these and one chips.' She disappears into the half-lit sodium stadium light. I can't get over him; just watching him order chips is a fantastic experience, just watching his mannerisms and listening to the sound of his strong Nigerian accent.

'This is such a big surprise,' Sidney says turning to me, and taking my hand in his. I'm drinking in his face. His face has the same shape as my own, his forehead is the same. I feel a strange almost ecstatic sensation of recognition. It is nearly primitive. I could happily sniff his ears and lick his forehead. It has completely ambushed me; I wasn't expecting it at all. 'What happened when you met my – ' Sidney corrects himself, '*our* father. Where was it again? Abuja?'

'Yes, he came by bus from Enugu to meet me at the Nicon Hotel. He said he'd a spiritual urge to meet me there. He prayed for me for two solid hours. At one point he kicked off his shoes and I recognized my own toes.'

Sidney nearly falls off his chair, laughing at this. 'I don't see it like our father sees it,' he says. 'It was a long time ago. It's not as if he was married then. He wasn't married. I'll talk to him and get him to see things differently. This is simple. It doesn't need to be complicated. No need to get stressed about things that don't need to be stressful.' I can't believe it. Sidney is the voice of reason.

'I think you might be underestimating how strongly your father . . .' I say.

'Please, *our* father!' Sidney interrupts.

'. . . feels. He sees me as his sin. He said when I met him, *if people were to know about you they would lose their faith in God.*'

'Nah,' Sidney says. 'I don't see it like that. The same blood flows in us.'

'Don't we look alike?' I ask Okey, who nods, charmed and moved by the whole encounter, sipping his beer gratefully and smoking a menthol cigarette.

'You two are so alike, you even have the same laugh,' Okey giggles.

Sidney holds my hand at the table, like he doesn't want to let go. I think he must feel the same as me, that recognition thing. 'This is your heritage,' Sidney says. 'You have a right. If our father dies and I say you must come and bury our father, what's going to happen? You're supposed to come to Nzagha and nobody knows who you are?'

I'm shocked by the speed Sidney has accepted me as his sister, right down to burial rites, *rights*. I've known about Sidney for years now. Until recently, I didn't know his name, but I did know I had three brothers and one sister. Sidney has only found out about me today and his response is categorical, certain, calm. Even though I'm a huge shock to him, he has no doubt about our connection. I'm not sure about burying Jonathan. I can't imagine being part of that, feeling part of it. It seems like another lifetime away, burying my African father. I drift off trying to imagine this other life, the one that I'd have had, had I been placed on the red dust road less travelled by, the one where I'd have been going to Nzagha every Christmas since I was born. It's alarming, the other life. It thrills and scares in equal measure because I would have never wanted to be without my mum and my dad, John and Helen, and can't imagine my life without them. It pains me to imagine that. 'I went to Nzagha!' I tell Sidney, hoping I'm pronouncing it right.

'You did?' he says, pleased. 'Did you see my bungalow, my twin bungalow? I share it with Amadi. He and I are so, so close.'

Sidney beams and his phone goes off. It is Amadi. Sidney talks so quickly to Amadi that I can't understand a single word of what he says. He passes the phone to me. 'Say hello to your brother,' he says.

'Kedu?' I say to Amadi shyly.

'Odimma,' Amadi says back, roaring with laughter. His laugh is the same laugh as Sidney's, as mine. 'This is amazing,' Amadi says on the phone. His voice is bubbling like champagne. 'I used to think I was number two, now

I am number three,' Amadi says. I try and imagine what he looks like, if he looks like Sidney.

'I can't wait to meet you too,' I say and hand the phone back to Sidney. Time is ticking.

'I've only told Amadi for now,' Sidney tells me. 'There is an order for things to happen. I'll fly to Enugu and talk to our father. I'll change his mind. I'll say this was in the past. He'll listen to me. Then I'll tell Ikenna and my sister.'

'What's her name?' She is the only one whose name I don't know. I had found out Sidney and Amadi and Ikenna. 'Chiamaka,' Sidney says and writes it down for me in my notebook.

'Actually she looks even more like you than I do,' he says. 'Wait till you see her. She's a herbalist. She took the same interest in trees and herbal cures as our father.'

'I knew she was an ethno-botanist, Jonathan let it slip when I met him, but he wouldn't say anybody's name. And Ikenna is the doctor?' He nods again, impressed this time. 'What does Amadi do?'

'He's an estate agent,' Sidney says. My world feels like it has expanded accordion-fashion and music is coming out blaring through the stadium speakers, a high-life mixture of Celtic and African music. I could dance a jig in a floodlit court. I'm at a fantastic celebration in the middle of a sports stadium; I feel that I've scored a goal, hooped a loop. I've tracked my brother down, and found him and together we could run round the red running track. He is overjoyed to meet me. Fancy that! He's not angry or suspicious or cautious. He is open-hearted, generous, kind. He is curious though about how I got his number. He asks me more than once. 'How did you get my number?' I don't know his name, I say, and I am actually telling the truth. He is a friend of a friend of a friend. Sidney laughs, good-naturedly. 'You are my sister. You are protecting your sources! I'll get it out of you when we know each other better.' He laughs again. There's so much laughter between us; it is passed back and forth like a basketball in the middle of a match. Every couple of minutes either the brother or the sister goes for a slam dunk.

'Amadi is more than my brother,' Sidney says. 'We are close in age. Close friends.'

I tell Sidney that I decided to contact him first, since he is the senior brother. 'You did the right thing. If you had contacted Ikenna first, he would have only come to me. They all defer to me. But now I will have to defer to you. You are my senior sister! If I want advice, you will have to give it.'

I nod, and gulp, trying to imagine that too, a new life suddenly filled with siblings wanting advice! I wonder if I'm up to it, and how tricky it all is. It's complicated. Tracing suddenly asks someone who has had one life to have two; and you can't have two lives, you can only have one. The empty ghost, the wraithlike figure that has stalked me for years seems to be taking off her pale polka-dot dress, slowly, in the sports stadium changing rooms, and hanging it onto a peg. She opens a locker, with her own key, found after years of fumbling, and disappears into its depths.

Sidney says, 'Isn't it funny, I always thought I was number one and now I realize I am number two.'

'Amadi just said that to me, that he always thought he was number two and now he's number three.'

Sidney looks blasted by the news, but euphoric. I'm not worried any more about whether or not I've done the right thing. It all feels right. It absolutely was the right thing to do. It is wonderful to clap my eyes on him and clasp his brotherly hand. I take my glasses off so that Sidney can see my eyes clearly. He notices, and takes his glasses off too. Our glasses, similar-shaped rectangle frames, lie on the table. Our eyes are the same shape.

'It's lovely to meet you,' I say to Sidney. 'But I'll understand if you don't want to meet again, once you've spoken to Jonathan. You might feel compromised.'

'No, no, no, no,' Sidney says to me. 'I am your serious brother. Are you my serious sister?'

The prawns come. Sidney shares them out, galvanized by the food and the shortage of time. We knock back our beer. Sidney has a Nigerian Guinness; I have a Gulder and Okey a Star beer. Our time is so short; it has all the nervous energy of extra time in a cup final; attention to minutes and seconds. Less than ten minutes to go. We've been together for forty minutes. 'You must be bright to have found me,' Sidney says, laughing. 'Thanks for persevering. How did you get my number?'

'I told you, I don't know his name.'

'Ah, Jackie, Jackie, protecting your sources, just like

me. You are my *sister*!' He laughs wildly. I laugh wildly too. So does Okey. We three in the dim-lit stadium cafe must look to the ordinary basketball player like a bunch of cackling witches.

'Have you met your mother often?' Sidney asks.

'No, four times only. She also doesn't want to tell her children. She's frightened.'

'What does she do?'

'She was a nurse when she met Jonathan. They met in a ballroom dance hall in Aberdeen.'

Sidney's eyes widen. 'It's amazing,' he says. 'It's good because this has enabled me to see him differently. He has a past I didn't know about and so . . . it has . . .'

'Opened him up?'

'Yes, exactly.'

When I get back home, it is this remark of Sidney's that glitters and shines, like a pebble washed over by the sea. I contemplate its speckled generosity, marvel at it, like it is a beautiful thing. I turn it over and over in my mind again and again. It is a marvel because I could never have anticipated it; I would never have guessed that that might have been Sidney's reaction. You spend so much time when tracing imagining people's possible reactions. But the fact is that for Sidney it has not shattered his vision of his father as I feared; it has enhanced it. Well, what do you know? He's implying that I've actually done him a service, a favour. Jonathan has emerged from this a more rounded man. I haven't, touch wood, damaged anything; I've blown life into it.

'I'm glad you see it like that,' I remember saying, though that didn't capture the half of what I felt.

'Yes, of course. It is in the past. It is yesterday. You can't do anything about yesterday but you can affect today and tomorrow.'

'Today and tomorrow and today,' I repeated like a mantra.

Our time is fast running out. Somebody will soon blow the whistle. Sidney tells me his birthday is January 17th. He was born in 1964. I am two years and two months older than him. He is forty-five. We've spent forty-five minutes together, a minute for every year. Sidney hugs me goodbye, and waves us off. When I get to Lagos International Airport Sidney is on the phone already. 'Safe flight home,' he says. 'I don't want to lose you already now that I've just found you.'

2009

I imagine Jonathan, already dressed in a brown jacket and yellow tie, headed for a meeting about plants in Enugu. He's walking fast. He is sprightly for a man of his years. His head is buzzing with cures. Someone stops him in the street to ask him if he can heal them. He stops to pray, pleased, and then continues walking the good, clean streets of Enugu. Today, God has arranged things well. And everything is going to plan. Soon, it will be Christmas and he'll meet with his family in the village. I imagine Elizabeth is already wearing her black-and-white checked coat and a winter scarf tied round her neck. She's been wearing her coat since six in the morning ready to go for church at ten. She's been sitting at her table clutching her black handbag which is crammed full of secrets. She won't let go of the bag. It comes everywhere with her. It is going to church. A minute ago she remembered she was going to church, and a minute later, she forgot.

She's driven to her church in a small car. When she gets inside, she relaxes. The hymns begin and she sings along. Once she used to sing Gaelic songs. Now, she stands on her feet and sings; the voices of the congregation rise and fall with her.

Glasgow

The first time I came back from Nigeria, I went home to Glasgow to tell my parents all about the meeting with Jonathan. I imitated him and danced round the living room in Bishopbriggs, clapping my hands, up to the ceiling and down to the floor, and doing the fancy footwork and putting on a deep incantatory Nigerian accent, '*You can walk through fire, you won't burn. You can cross the waters, you won't drown. Don't even bother with your hotel safe.*'

My mum sat on her favourite armchair and kicked her legs in the air, she was laughing so much. 'What a scream, what an absolute scream. See your life. You couldn't make it up.' The tears poured down her face. 'That's given me the biggest laugh.'

My dad shook his head and said, 'You're no bad at doing that accent.'

I showed them both the photographs I'd taken of Jonathan in his white lace dress, and ornate trousers, and my mum said, 'Where's he getting all the regalia?' Then she said, 'He mibbe looks a bit like you across the forehead.'

My dad studied the photograph of my father and said, 'I canny see it. I canny see any resemblance at all.'

This time, when I come back from Nigeria, I go to visit my parents and tell them all about meeting Sidney. My mum's excited again, but not as much as the last time. 'How do you think this story compares with the last?' she says. She hasn't kicked her legs in the air. Then she says, 'What is he to me? What relation is he to me? What am I to call him?'

I think for a moment and say, 'He can call you his Scottish mum.'

'I like it. I like it,' my mum says.

My dad says, jokingly, 'If he's coming over here, he better get his ain job, because I canny support any mair.'

I show them the photograph of Sidney and me that Okey took in the stadium. 'Oh my,' my mum says, 'he's your spit. He's your double.'

'Ye can definitely see a likeness,' my dad says. 'Oh Christ, aye.'

Later that Saturday afternoon my brother arrives and I show him the photograph. 'Your brother's coal black,' my brother says. 'Coal black, eh?'

'He's going to come and visit,' I tell them.

'Oh lovely,' my mum says. 'Isn't it amazing how rich life is, how our family's expanding? Just incredible!'

My dad looks a little uncomfortable with this statement, as if he'd very much prefer his family to stay exactly as it is, but he nods, generously, and says nothing.

My mum says, 'Maybe one year you'll be spending Christmas in Nigeria!' My dad looks a little dismayed.

'Oh no, I'd never do that,' I say. 'I love you and Dad coming for Christmas.'

'It'll not be long now till Matthew's back,' my mum says.

'I can't wait,' I say. Matthew's been away in Guadalajara for four months now. 'I miss my boy.'

When I emailed Sidney pictures of my family, he said, 'Your son is really tall.'

'Yes, he's six foot two.' I told Sidney that once Matthew had given me a hug and said to me, 'Mum, if I stand at my full height and give you a hug, I feel like I'm consoling a small child.'

Sidney laughed wildly. 'So he has a sense of humour too?'

'Oh yes,' I said, 'he's very droll and dry.'

'Do you remember that time when you came down to stay in London and Matthew was just two years old?' I say to my dad. 'And I said to Matthew, "Go and watch Grandpa shave," because I felt that he was being a little deprived having no man in the house. And he went and watched you shave and when he came back down, I said, "Did you watch Grandpa shave," and Matthew said, "Yeeees, but he didn't do it properly, he only went like this," Matthew made scraping motions with his hand under his chin, "he didn't do it properly, he didn't do his legs."'

'That's right,' my dad says, laughing at the memory.

'And remember that time when you got into the car to drive and Matthew was about three and he said to you, "Men don't drive," and you said, "Aye they do, *men drive*!" And then you said to me, "You'll need to be careful you're not bringing up that boy in too esoteric a household."'

'Is that what I says to you?' my dad says, laughing. 'I doubt I said that. You bloody writers, you make so much up.'

'No, you definitely said it,' I say, 'because I remember the phrase. It's memorable, *esoteric household*.'

'Ah well, I said it if you say so,' my dad says, reluctantly, wryly. 'Aye, he came oot wey good wan liners, Matthew.' My dad is proud of his six-foot-two grandson. 'When's he coming hame?'

'Christmas Eve. He'll be back the day after you arrive.'

'Good. Good,' my dad says.

'Oh, I'm looking forward to my Christmas,' my mum says.

The next morning, a Sunday, my mum comes down the stairs with her dressing gown on, rubbing her back. 'I've an awful sore back,' she says. 'It must have been giving birth in the night, to my forty-five-year-old Nigerian son.'

That afternoon I call Sidney from Glasgow and tell him my mum is to be called his Scottish mum. Sidney says, 'She doesn't mind? She doesn't mind about me?'

'No,' I say. 'She's delighted; she says her family is expanding.'

'Nice,' Sidney says, laughing. 'I like it. Are you going to church today?'

'No, I'm not going to church,' I say, the church bells ringing in my head, remembering the time when to rebel I said the whole of the Lord's Prayer aloud to my mum and dad to wind them up, and then made my mum come to church with me, when I was in the church choir. I was seven. 'I had to buy a hat specially,' my mum is always saying, like it was some big trauma. 'So you did.' (My religious period lasted three weeks. I managed to stay in the Brownies a little longer, four weeks, but then the jokes about a brown Brownie didn't help.)

'Do you remember I was in the socialist Sunday School choir?' I say to my dad and he nods.

'I sang all those songs, "Down by the Riverside", and If I had a hammer, I'd hammer in the morning, I'd hammer in the evening, All over this land.'

'Aye and you still canny sing,' my mum says, laughing.

My dad continues, 'I'd hammer out danger, I'd hammer out a warning, I'd hammer out love between my brothers and my sisters, all over this land.'

'And then there's the bell,' my mum says. 'How does it end?'

'Well, I've got a hammer and I've got a bell and I've got a song to sing, All over this land. It's the hammer of justice, it's the bell of freedom, And it's the song about love between my brothers and my sisters all over this land,' my dad sings, a singing reply to my mum's question. My dad and mum have started to dance round the living room. 'Come on, Jackie, on your feet!' I dance with them, as I've danced so many times before, up and down our small stage. I think of my brothers and my sisters. What my life would have been like if I'd grown up with my sisters and brother in Milton Keynes, what it would have been like if I'd grown up with my brothers and sister in Enugu. What *I* would have been like, what job I might have done, if I'd have been a nurse, a hairdresser or an ethno-botanist, or if I'd still have been a writer. I don't imagine I would have been a writer. I can't imagine my life any other way than the way I've lived it. In my parents' house back from Nigeria, I feel flooded with love for them; it is like the light across the land, the moon light on the night fields. I think of my friend's comment years ago, 'You should be grateful that they adopted you,' and my mum's anger, 'Don't let anyone tell you to be grateful.' And though I know what she meant, my mum, and would still mean, I *am* grateful to have grown up in the house with John and Helen Kay to have had them, great humanitarians that they are, as my mum and my dad. A line from the only letter Jonathan ever wrote me comes back to me, freshly made and minted, 'I thank God for your adoptive parents,' and I think that he, too, has not been without generosity. 'Remain blessed,' was the last line of the letter, I remember. And I do, I am, I do feel blessed.

'Are you wanting a bowl of this soup?' my dad asks me.

'Yes, please,' I say, and he ladles me out a generous portion of his own home-made Scotch broth. 'Is that all right for you?'

'Delicious!' I say.

'I'm not hungry,' my mum says, refusing my dad's offer of soup. 'I'm feeling thon way.'

The greenhouse that my brother is building for my mum is nearly finished in the garden. 'Do you see my greenhouse?' my mum says, happily. 'I'm going to grow tomatoes.'

2009

I go back to Quarry Bank Mill. I want to find another tree with a secret hollow. I walk the dog past the old mill house and take the path up to the right. It is fairly steep. The trees are golden, autumnal, their amber warmth lifts me. I'm back here again. I've found one brother and met him. One day I might meet my other brothers and sisters. The leaves on the trees are every variation of orange, every possible colour between red and yellow: burnt orange, tangerine, russet orange. A little woman passes me. She sees me looking at the trees. 'A lot of leaves yet to fall before winter,' she says and walks on. Right now, in their glory and amber abundance, it's impossible to imagine them bare. Impossible to imagine every single leaf still left to fall and fall and fall. They are too vivacious and splendid. I find an old oak tree with a perfect hollow and slip my golden coin in. The hollow opens its dark mouth and swallows my golden coin whole.

The autumn sun shines through the trees like a blessing. I follow the path up and up and up. The golden gift of the late autumn sunlight warms my back. I like the sound of the leaves crunching under my feet. It is a lucky sound. I decide that next week I will soak the moringa pods Uncle Nwora gave me and try my luck at growing a *Moringa oleifera* tree. I have never been particularly green-fingered, but you never know the minute. They are hardy trees, put the pods directly into the soil, Uncle Nwora said. I will chance my luck. I'll plant the tree to mark meeting my brother Sidney, like my mum fifty years ago, planted the cherry blossom to celebrate adopting my brother Maxwell.

I try and imagine my own moringa growing in the front garden of my terraced house in Manchester, far away from its home. I wonder if the pods will ever take root. I picture my healthy, tall moringa in ten years' time. Will I still be living here then? I imagine a magical moringa, years and years away from now; its roots have happily absorbed and transported water and minerals from the dark, moist soil to the rest of the splendid tree.

Acknowledgements

Thank you to all the people in this book.
Thank you, Pat Kavanagh, Ian Jack, Kate Harvey,
Camilla Elworthy and Sarah Chalfant.